ON THE TWO WAYS

Life or Death, Light or Darkness:
Foundational Texts in the Tradition

ST VLADIMIR'S SEMINARY PRESS
Popular Patristics Series
Number 41

The Popular Patristics Series published by St Vladimir's Seminary Press provides readable and accurate translations of a wide range of early Christian literature to a wide audience—students of Christian history to lay Christians reading for spiritual benefit. Recognized scholars in their fields provide short but comprehensive and clear introductions to the material. The texts include classics of Christian literature, thematic volumes, collections of homilies, letters on spiritual counsel, and poetical works from a variety of geographical contexts and historical backgrounds. The mission of the series is to mine the riches of the early Church and to make these treasures available to all.

Series Editor
BOGDAN BUCUR

Associate Editor
IGNATIUS GREEN

* * *

Series Editor
1999–2020
JOHN BEHR

On the
Two Ways

LIFE OR DEATH, LIGHT OR DARKNESS:
FOUNDATIONAL TEXTS IN THE TRADITION

Edited by
ALISTAIR STEWART(-SYKES)

ST VLADIMIR'S SEMINARY PRESS
YONKERS, NEW YORK
2011

Library of Congress Cataloging-in-Publication Data

On the two ways : life or death, light or darkness : foundation texts in the tradition / edited by Alistair Stewart-Sykes.

p. cm. — (St. Vladimir's Seminary Press's "popular patristics" series ; no. 41)

Includes bibliographical references.

ISBN 978–0–88141–850–7

1. Christian life—History—Sources. 2. Good and evil—Religious aspects—Christianity—History of doctrines—Sources. I. Stewart-Sykes, Alistair.

BV4490.O5 2011
248.09—dc22

2010029801

COPYRIGHT © 2011 BY

ST VLADIMIR'S SEMINARY PRESS
575 Scarsdale Road, Yonkers, NY 10707
1-800-204-2665
www.svspress.com

ISBN 978–0–88141–850–7
ISSN 1555–5755

PRINTED IN THE UNITED STATES OF AMERICA

For James and Aidan
my Godsons

Abbreviations List

B	*The Epistle of Barnabas*
β	A hypothetical source for the Two Ways as found in B
D	The *Didache*
δ	A hypothetical source for the Two Ways as found in D and L.
E	The summary of the commands of the apostles of catholic tradition (also known as the *Epitome*).
K	The *Apostolic Church Order*
κ	A hypothetical version of the Two Ways as found in K and E
L	The Teaching of the apostles, a Latin version of the Two Ways
TWT	The Two Ways Tradition

Contents

Preface

In the early years of the common era, as Judaism and Christianity each emerged, their adherents saw that life presents us with a choice of following one of two ways, either of goodness or of evil, characterized variously as ways of life or death, of light or darkness, of truth or deceit. This conviction is presented to us in a number of different versions and literary contexts. This book contains various presentations of these two ways from across the centuries. Some of the ground has been trodden well before whereas some is virtually uncharted territory. I must stress, however, that this is a book for the novice and not for the seasoned explorer.

Beyond presenting the material the editor faces two tasks. First, the context for the various presentations of the two ways needs to be established; in some cases it is clear, in others less so. In any event the contexts vary from a manual for the direction of converts to monastic rules to literary exercises. Second, the literary relationship which obtains between the various versions needs to be sought out. In this way we may see the way in which early Christians used the material which had come to them, ultimately from Scripture, and found ways in which to apply this material to their needs and circumstances. Thus when the two-ways material is presented the whole works in which the two-ways material is found have been included, as far as is practicable. When a work drawing on the tradition is of a length which precludes inclusion in a work of this size, at least a context is given. This enables us to explore the content and the life of this long-lived tradition.

Annotation is kept to a minimum. Not even every scriptural allusion is noted, in particular because we cannot be sure, especially in the case of the earlier documents, whether the apparent allusion is taken from a written Gospel or from oral tradition. Therefore references are given only where a direct citation is clearly intended. Citations are given according to the Septuagint, even though, particularly in the case of the *Epistle of Barnabas*, there may be a great deal of divergence from the received text.

I would encourage readers whose interest is aroused by the tradition to explore further, and so I conclude these prefatory remarks with some suggestions for further reading. Principal among this reading should be confrontation with the texts themselves. The following editions are employed, many of which have extensive notes and introductions. The only textual notes in the present work are points at which I have deviated from the published texts, or seriously considered so doing. Where I am aware that commentaries and introductions in English are available, these are also noted, even if the texts have not been the basis of the versions here. Some of these works have been translated many times before, but the material from the *Life of Shenoute* has never previously been translated directly into English, and the ps-Athanasian material has, to my knowledge, never been translated into a modern language.

Didache: Ed. W. Rordorf, A. Tuilier, *La doctrine des douze apôtres* (2nd ed.; SC 248; Paris: Cerf, 1998). A new work on this text is currently being produced by Jonathan Draper, for publication by Oxford University Press, and is sure to be a standard work for the English reader. For the moment note K. Niederwimmer *The Didache* (Minneapolis: Fortress, 1998) and Aaron Milavec, *The Didache: faith, hope and life of the earliest Christian communities* (New York: Newman, 2003), both of which have significant strengths and weaknesses.

Doctrina apostolorum: Ed. Rordorf and Tuilier *Doctrine*, 207–210.

Epistle of Barnabas: Ed. R.A. Kraft, in Pierre Prigent, R.A. Kraft, *Épître de Barnabé* (SC 172: Paris: Cerf, 1971). For an English version with introduction and notes see R.A. Kraft, *The Apostolic Fathers 3: Barnabas and the Didache* (New York: Nelson, 1965).

Apostolic Church Order: Ed. A. Stewart-Sykes *The Apostolic Church Order* (Sydney: St Paul's, 2006). Has an extensive introduction and brief notes.

Epitome: Ed. Theodor Schermann, *Eine Elfapostelmoral oder die X-Rezension der "beiden Wege"* (Munich: Lentner, 1903), 16–18. This text is reprinted in Stewart-Sykes, *Apostolic Church Order*.

Life of Shenoute: Ed. E. Amélineau, *Monuments pour servir à l'histoire de l'Égypte chrétienne aux IVe et Ve siècles* (Paris: Ernest Leroux, 1888), 291–296.

Syntagma doctrinae: Ed. P. Battifol, in *Syntagma doctrinae* (Studia Patristica 2; Paris: Ernest Leroux, 1890)

Fides patrum: Ed. P. Battifol, *Didascalia CCCXVIII patrum* (Paris: Ernest Leroux, 1887). Battifol also published this text as "Canones Nicaeni pseudepigraphi" in *Revue Archeologique* (3rd series) 6 (1885), 133–141.

Rule of St Benedict: Ed. anon. (Montecassino: np, 1959). I believe that many versions and texts are available, but have no expertise in this area.

ps-Boniface: Ed. H. van de Sandt and D. Flusser in *The Didache: Its Jewish Sources and its Place in early Judaism and Christianity* (Assen: Van Gorcum, 2002), 102–103. The chapter also contains an introduction.

The Second Catechesis of the Manner of Catechizing Converts: Ed. van de Sandt and Flusser, *Didache*, 109. The text is introduced with some comment.

I have profited much from discussion of these texts with many people, both in England and in the low countries, and from reading much literature which is not acknowledged directly in the notes. A particular debt, however, which must be acknowledged, is to Posy Clayton of the neighbouring parish of Spetisbury, who is responsible for the translation of the section from the *Life of Shenoute*. The value of this book is much enhanced by the appearance of this material.

May the dedicatees, and all who read my work, walk in the way of light!

Sturminster Marshall Vicarage: On the Feast of the Epiphany 2008

CHAPTER ONE

The two ways in forming Judaism

PART ONE:
THE GENESIS OF THE TWO WAYS TRADITION

Before the Israelites entered the land of promise, Moses, according to the Deuteronomist, addressed them, setting forth the commandments of God, and stating that he was setting before the people a blessing and a curse, a blessing which would come about if the people were obedient to the commandments and the curse which would come about if they turned away from those commandments and followed other gods.[1]

This bifurcation of ways may be recognized likewise within the Scriptures of the old covenant in the first Psalm, which sets forth the way of the one who is blessed in obedience in contrast to the way of the wicked, and in the story of Jeremiah who is instructed by the Lord to tell the people of Jerusalem to surrender. The way of surrender would be a way of life, whereas remaining in the city would be a way of death.[2]

This fundamental idea seems to have grown in developing Judaism and particularly in the ethical instruction of Jewish teachers. Thus in the *Testaments of the Twelve Patriarchs* we read in the *Testament of Levi* 19 that we are to choose for ourselves light or darkness, and in the *Testament of Asher* 1.6–8 that there are two ways, of good and evil, and alongside these are two impulses in the human heart.

[1]Deut 11.27–28.
[2]Jer 21.8–9.

The two ways thus form an ethical discourse setting out the two ways of life and death, of light and darkness, embedded in early Jewish ethical teaching. Apart from the arrangement of two ways, much of the material to be found within the presentation of the two ways is found in other Jewish writings, such as the ethical poem of ps-Phocylides, a Jewish work from around the turn of the common era setting forth ideals for wisdom and conduct. In turn we may note that much of this material, as was the original idea of a fundamental choice between life and death, was rooted within Scripture, but these are made real in their presentation within the forming Judaism of the centuries around the turn of the common era.

Thus when candidates sought admission to the group of covenanters at Qumran, their instructor was directed to instruct them in the two ways, over which angels were set, the ways of darkness and light. This statement in the *Community Rule* enables us to see that this group[3] saw themselves as a community in covenant with God and distinct from other forms of Judaism as from any non-Jewish culture. This rule sets out the regulations by which the community is managed but begins with a statement of covenant renewal and then sets forth the two ways. As such the whole is seen in an overall covenantal context as the means by which the instructor of the community is to direct the covenantal basis of the group.

We may read the discourse regarding the two ways as it was presented to those seeking admission into this group.

> It is for the instructor to make all the sons of light to understand and to train them regarding all the generations of the sons of men, regarding the various spirits, regarding their distinguishing signs, concerning their deeds in their societies and concerning the visitation of their punishments together

[3]We will not enter here into the discussion as to whether the group was Essene, and the relationship between this group and the caves in which the scrolls were found. It is sufficient for our purpose that the group which produced the *Community Rule* was a group within early Judaism.

with their final rewards. All that is and all that shall be is from the God of knowledge, and he prepared their entire design. When they have come into being, at their appointed time, they will perform their actions in accordance with his glorious design without any possibility of change. Laws for all are in his hands and he supplies all their needs. He created humanity to have governance over the earth and set within him two spirits so that he would walk with them until the time of his visitation. These are the spirits of truth and of deceit. From the spring of light come the generations of truth and from the well of darkness come the generations of deceit. In the hand of the prince of lights is governance over the sons of righteousness, and they walk in the way of light, and in the hand of the angel of darkness is total governance over the sons of deceit and they walk in the ways of darkness. All the corruption of the sons of light is from the angel of darkness, and all their sins and their wickedness, their guilt and their misdeeds are in his governance in accordance with the mysteries of God until it is his time. All their afflictions and the occasions of their troubles are caused by the governance of his hostility and all the spirits of his inheritance cause the sons of light to fall. The God of Israel and the angels of his truth assist all the sons of light. He created the spirits of light and darkness and set every deed upon them, and on their ways every labour.[4] God loves one of them for all eternity and delights in all his deeds. The other he despises. He hates his counsel and all his ways for ever.

These are their ways in the world: to illuminate the human heart and to make straight before him all the ways of true justice, and to implant fear of the precepts of God within his heart. It is a spirit of humility, patience, generous compassion, eternal goodness, prudence, discernment, and powerful wisdom which trusts entirely to the deeds of

[4]The phrase "and on their ways every labour" is erroneously repeated in the MS.

God and rests upon the abundance of his mercies, a spirit knowledgeable in every plan to act and zealous for the precepts of righteousness, of holy plans with fixed purpose, and abundance of mercies for all the sons of truth, of glorious purity which despises all unclean idols, of self-effacing and cautious conduct in everything, concealing the mysteries of knowledge on account of the truth. These are the fixings for the sons of truth (in) the world. The reward for all who walk in them is healing, plentiful peace through a length of days, fruitful offspring with everlasting blessings, leading to endless enjoyment in everlasting life and a crown of glory with majestic clothing in everlasting light.

To the spirit of deceit belong arrogance of life and idleness in the service of righteousness, evil and lying, pride and haughtiness of heart, falsehood and cruel treachery, much hypocrisy, impatience, much folly and zeal for the performance of abominable deeds in a spirit of lust and filthy ways in the service of impurity, a blasphemous tongue, eyes blinded, ears stopped, neck stiff and heart hardened in walking in all the ways of darkness and of trickery. The reward for all who walk in it will be great affliction at the hands of all the angels of destruction, with eternal damnation from the burning rage of the God of vengeance, for endless terror and unending shame, reproached in their destruction by fire in darkness. To the end of their generations in bitter weeping and with harsh evils in the abysses of darkness until their annihilation . . . no remnant or survivor for them.

In these are the generations of all the children of men and according to their divisions all their forces have a share in their history and walk in their ways and all the deeds which they perform are in their division, in accordance with what anyone's birth-right might be, either great or small, to all the eternal ages. For God has sorted them into equal parts until the last time, and has put an everlasting hatred between their divisions. Deeds of deceit are abhorrent to truth and all ways of truth are abhorrent to deceit. The conflict between their precepts is ferocious, as they will not walk together. In the mystery of his knowledge and the glory of his wisdom God has appointed an end to lifetime of deceit, and will wipe it out for ever. At that time shall truth rise up (in) the world, for it has been defiled in the ways of wickedness during the dominion of deceit until the occasion of the determined judgement. Then will God refine with his truth every human deed and will purify for himself people's inner parts, tearing out from within their flesh every spirit of deceit and cleansing them from every wicked deed with the spirit of holiness. He will sprinkle them with the spirit of truth like cleansing water (to cleanse them) from all the abomination of falsehood and from the defilement of the unclean spirit, so to instruct those who are upright in the knowledge of the most high and to give the understanding of the children of heaven to those whose way is perfect. God has chosen them for an everlasting covenant, and theirs shall be all the glory of Adam. Deceit shall be no more and all the deeds of trickery shall be put to shame. Until now the spirits of truth and of deceit are struggling within the human heart. They walk in wisdom or in folly. In accordance with a person's share in the truth he shall be righteous and abhor injustice, and according to his share in deceit shall he act wickedly and abhor the truth. For God has sorted them into equal parts until the end and the new beginning. He knows the outcome of their deeds for all times and everlastingly and has given them to the children of men that they might know good [and evil] and has assigned the lots of all that live in accordance with their spirit until [the occasion of] his visitation. (1 QS [*Community Rule*] 3.13–4.26)[5]

[5]Translated by the editor from the text provided by Florentino García Martínez and Eibert J.C. Tigchelaar, *The Dead Sea Scrolls: Study Edition* I (Leiden: Brill, 1997).

As Christianity was born as a distinct faith within the matrix of early Jewish practices and beliefs, the teaching of two ways became part of early Christian discourse as well, and so is found in a number of Christian documents. One should not press the parallels between this version of the two ways and those which are found in early Christianity too closely, but there is a noticeable literary similarity in that two ways are presented and the outline of the two ways is laid out, the way of life and light preceding the way of darkness and death. We may also note a conceptual parallel between this and many Christian presentations of the two ways in that the ways are seen as the outcome of a covenant which the individual is called to make with God. As the work proceeds we will suggest that this idea is fundamental to the emerging Two Ways Tradition (TWT).

It was the observation of the links between this section of the *Community Rule* and early Christian presentations of the two ways which proved that the two-ways literature had itself been formed within a Jewish matrix.[6] This had been suspected beforehand, but there were many other hypotheses about the genesis of the form. The identification of the form within the *Community Rule* demonstrates that the form was part at least of the currency of forming Judaism and that it is from such a source that it was adopted by Christians. One should not, however, be misled into making the presentation in the *Community Rule* determinative for other possible Jewish presentations. In particular, both the cosmological dualism which characterizes this presentation and the deterministic tendencies may be peculiarities of the group which produced it. Nonetheless the covenantal context of the presentation may be more generally shared, not simply because this conception is so basic to early Judaism, whatever its form, but in that such a context may be seen as the genesis of other presentations, deriving from its scriptural antecedent. Thus when Levi tells his sons to choose either darkness or light

---

[6] Through the classic work of J.-P. Audet, "Affinités littéraires et doctrinales du 'Manuel de discipline'" *Revue Biblique* 59 (1952), 219–238.

he defines these ways as the law of God or the works of Beliar;[7] likewise *Testament of Asher* defines the way of light as following in the law of God.[8] From its onset the teaching of the two ways was understood as an expansion of the nature of the covenantal relationship between the follower and God.

This was an inner-Jewish movement; whether this pattern was employed for the instruction of gentile proselytes we cannot know. What we may discern, however, is that when it was adopted by early Christian groups, which were founded within Judaism, it was put to that purpose. Not only the context of pre-baptismal instruction in which it is found in the *Didache*, an early Christian document presented in the next chapter, but also the contents themselves betray an eye to the disjunction between Jewish law and gentile mores. This becomes clear from an examination of the contents of the tradition as it is delivered to us.

PART TWO: THE CONTENTS OF THE JEWISH AND CHRISTIAN TWO WAYS TRADITION

For the most part the contents of the Christian two ways are self-explanatory. However a brief summary, which may serve as a commentary on all the materials which these documents hold in common, may nonetheless be useful, in particular in enabling us to see what is distinct about this ethic within the Hellenistic world, and the extent to which the tradition draws upon the *lingua franca* of Jewish ethical discourse.

The *Didache* (henceforth termed **D**) is taken as the source for this summary as it is the most extensive of the presentations, and presents the material in an order which is common to a number of other Christian presentations, including later Christian adaptations of the material. This does not mean that any privileged position is

[7] *Testament of Levi* 19.1.
[8] *Testament of Asher* 6.

given to **D**, indeed we shall observe that it is itself a developed form within Christian discourse, but it enables us nonetheless to understand the impact that the discourse deriving from Judaism might make upon a gentile audience.

The material starts with a statement of the two ways, of life and of death (**D** 1.1).

The opening of the way of life is a twofold statement of the command to love God and one's neighbour (**D** 1.2). Such a double commandment is found in the Gospels, but this need not be the source, as contemporary Judaism likewise promulgated a double commandment as a summary of the law. We may note, as examples:

> Therefore, my children, keep the law of the Lord, act in simplicity and walk guilelessly. Do not enquire into God's commands and your neighbour's business, but love God and your neighbour and show compassion to the poor and the weak. (*Testament of Issachar* 5.1–2)

> Love the Lord through all your life, and one another with a true heart. (*Testament of Dan* 5.3)

> Before he (an Essene initiate) may touch the common food he is made to swear grave oaths, firstly of reverence towards the divine, and then to preserve justice towards people ... (Josephus, *Jewish War* 2.139)

Of the many, so to speak, particular principles and tenets (studied in the synagogue) two headings stand out; duty towards God through reverence, and sanctity and duty towards people through humanity and justice. (Philo, *Special Laws* 2.63)

TWT is thus in the mainstream of Judaism in setting this double commandment at the head.

It is then expanded by a declaration of how one actually might love one's neighbour through the statement of the golden rule. (**D**

1.2) Again, this is a commonplace expression in Jewish literature, as for instance, Tobit 4:15: "Do to no one what you yourself dislike."

The passage which follows, ***D*** 1.3–6, is known as the "Gospel section" because it is largely paralleled within the Gospels, and most especially Matthew's sermon on the mount, as it treats the need to love enemies and not to seek revenge for wrongs. We shall see, however, that this section is unique to ***D*** amongst the documents containing the two ways. We shall not join the debate here about the nature of the relationship between the material found in this section and that found within the synoptic tradition but may note, once again, the possibility of a mainstream Jewish source behind some of the components at least, such as Prov. 25:21, "If your enemy is hungry, feed him. If he is thirsty, give him water to drink," and *Testament of Benjamin* 5.4: "Anyone who does injury to a holy man shall be repentant, as the holy man shall take pity on the offender and be silent."

Within the Gospel section the statement that one should love one's neighbour is noted to include enemies, and this in turn is expanded by a discussion of the manner in which one should respond to hostility. A statement about giving (***D*** 1.5) is then likewise expanded, again using traditional material. The traditional nature of the expansion may be illustrated from Hermas *Mandate* 2.4–6, ". . . give simply, not distinguishing between those to whom you should give and those to whom you should not give . . . Those who received shall give an account to God as what they received and for what purpose . . . The giver is therefore innocent . . . " This outlook also has a background nestling in Judaism. Thus see ps-Phocylides 29–30: "Give to the needy of those things that God has given you; let all of life be in common and all things be in agreement" and *Testament of Zabulon* 7.2: "Give to all with a good heart." The saying about alms sweating in the hand, with which the section concludes, then amends the statement, though it is less easy to place. Nonetheless we may observe Sirach 12.1 "If you do good, know who it is to whom you do it" and ps-Phocylides 23: "Fill up your hand and give alms to the needy." In general we may see this expansion to the tradition as a clarification of the matter of how it is that the second precept of the double commandment is properly to be fulfilled.

After this the tradition is picked up again with a free treatment of the commandments of the second table of the Decalogue (*D* 2.1–7). These are expanded, however, and given further exposition. We may note a few as being particularly significant.

First we may note the expansion of the ban on adultery to include pederasty. Whereas this practice is shunned absolutely within Judaism there is ample evidence that sexual relations between men and boys, much celebrated within the classical period, continued not only to occur but to be idealized within the Hellenistic world well into the common era. We may note the collections of epigrams on beautiful boys by Straton of Samos within the twelfth book of the Greek anthology, as well as the more comic presentation within Lucian's *Dialogues of the Courtesans* 10, in which a philosophy master prevents his pupil from seeing women as a means of gaining sexual favours for himself.

Secondly we may note the ban on abortion and exposure as an extension of the commandment not to kill. These practices were far from unknown in the contemporary world, and so the author might well see it as necessary to clarify the scope of the commandment to cover the unborn and the newly born. On the practice of abortion note Juvenal, *Satire* 6.595–597, Ovid. *Loves* 2.13 and 14, both of which take a negative view of the practice even while bearing witness to it. On exposure note the comments of Pliny, *Letter* 10.65–6, and 72, concerned at various issues raised by those who, having been exposed, are rescued and need support, and Plutarch, *On the Love of Offspring* 497E, which views with sympathy the situation of the poor man forced to expose a child. Both practices are widely condemned within Judaism, and Aristotle (*Zoica*, Fragment 283) finds it remarkable that Jews rear all their children.

There were a variety of motives and justifications offered for abortion and infanticide in the ancient world but, but whatever their rationale, they are seen by the TWT as breaches of the commandment not to kill. A gentile might not see that, and so what may be obvious to us, but not to the original audience, is pointed out.

This discussion of the second table of the Decalogue is then interrupted by another section, known as the *teknon* sayings, as they are introduced by the saying "Child, or "My child."[9] (*D* 3.1–6) The nature of this address from a teacher indicates a catechetical origin, and the tendency amongst them all is to illustrate the extent to which minor foibles might, unchecked, become major sins. Although there are some parallels within Jewish literature, such as the extended treatment of the *Testament of Dan* on the dangers of anger, Sirach 23.4b–5a on adultery (cf. *Testament of Benjamin* 8.2, which states that the man who is pure in heart does not look lecherously upon a woman), and 1 QS 1.6 on curiosity leading to idolatry, these insights are not so culturally embedded as those which precede. The most compelling parallels are, however, to be found in a late talmudic work, the *Derekh 'eretz zuta*. For instance: "The first stage of vowing leads to folly; the first stage of uncleanness leads to idolatry; the first stage of levity with women leads to unchastity"[10] or "Do not let your ears listen to idle chatter, because they are the first of the organs to be burnt."[11] It is possible that the two indeed share a common ancestor; it is noteworthy that, just as this *teknon* section may have a scholastic origin, so the *Derekh 'eretz zuta* is addressed to those aspiring to be scholars. Unusually for a talmudic work the sayings are not attributed to rabbis, and whatever the age of the collection, the contents have obtained a proverbial status and so may even precede the Tannaim. The *teknon* section may thus have been formed quite independently of the TWT in a Jewish environment, even though its insights are not tied to Jewish practice.

We will note below that this section is not found in at least one early Christian manifestation of the TWT, and may represent a

[9]"Teknon" is Greek for child.
[10]*Derekh 'eretz zuta* 3.6.
[11]*Derekh 'eretz zuta* 5.6.

development on the level of what we shall come to recognize as the δ redaction, a version of TWT employed by *D* and by other Christian forms of the material.

The next section (*D* 3.7–10), describes an ideal of meekness and humility. Niederwimmer sums up a long tradition of interpretation in suggesting that this sets forth the ideal of the poor derived from the Hebrew Scriptures.[12] But Kloppenborg has recently pointed out that the citation that "the meek shall inherit the earth" from Ps 36.11 is to be contrasted with the manner in which the Qumran sectaries interpreted the verse, namely as the vindication of the poor at the end of time. Rather, he suggests, advice to associate with the lowly is addressed to those who have a choice about those with whom they might associate, and who would be in a position to associate with the exalted. Rather than being taken as addressed to the poor, this is addressed to those of relatively high social status. Like the foregoing section, and that which follows, this is advice which has its origin in the instruction of students. Thus he compares this passage to *Testament of Dan* 6.9: "For he (the father of the nations) is true and patient and mild and lowly, and teaches through his works the law of God."[13] We may note that advice to associate with the lowly and not with the exalted is counter-cultural in the extreme when addressed to gentiles. One may recall Juvenal's picture at *Satire* 3.126–132, of Romans pressing around the powerful and wealthy in the hope of recognition and some favour.

D then (at 4.1–12) moves on to what, at first sight, might appear to be a *Haustafel*, a list of household duties and responsibilities. But it is interesting that the primary concern is that the one instructed might support the teacher. The statement that one should remember one's teacher "night and day" may be contrasted to the suggestion that it is the coming judgement which is constantly to be recalled

[12]K. Niederwimmer *The Didache* (Minneapolis: Fortress, 1998), 100–102.

[13]John S. Kloppenborg, "Poverty and piety in Matthew, James and the Didache" in Huub van de Sandt and Jürgen K.. Zangenberg (edd.) *Matthew, James and the Didache: three related documents in their Jewish and Christian settings* (Atlanta: SBL, 2008), 201–232 at 218–222.

within the version of the two ways found in the *Epistle of Barnabas*. This distinction seems to have excited surprisingly little comment, although Peterson was so exercised by it that he suspected a corrupt text in *D*.[14] Other, following, instructions may perhaps be read in the light of the first direction to remember one's teacher. For instance the instruction that whoever has something to give should give it may perhaps be read in the light of what had come before, namely that there is an expectation that the teacher should receive economic support. Significantly more instruction is addressed to somebody who might own slaves than to slaves themselves, who appear as something of an afterthought. The statement that the teacher might be feared even as heaven is found in M. *Abot* 4.12, but this is attributed to R. Eleazar b. Shammua, a disciple of Aqiba, and so is almost certainly later than *D* in formation. It seems that as, in this (Christian?) community as certainly in some Jewish communities, the role of teachers begins to come to prominence, so the necessity that they be supported also comes about. Even references to schism and to judgement may be read as the avoidance of schism through the avoidance of dispute, and just judgement as the judgement of the content of teaching and in the discernment of prophecy.

The conclusion to the way of life (*D* 4.13–14) is almost formulaic, with its insistence that no commandment be abandoned, nor the content of the instruction altered. The root is probably Deut 4.2, "You shall not add to the word that I speak to you, neither shall you take away from it: keep the commandments of the Lord your God which I command you," but we may also note 1 Enoch 104.10–13, *Letter of Aristeas,* in which agreement to the excellence of the translation of the Septuagint is greeted with a curse on anyone who added, altered or subtracted from it, and Josephus, *Antiquities* 1.17.

---

[14]E. Peterson, "Über einige Probleme der Didache-Überlieferung," in *Frühkirche, Judentum und Gnosis* (Rome: Herder, 1959), 146–182, at 153–154. Cf., however, E. Hennecke, "Die Grundschrift der Didache und ihre Recensionen," *ZNW* 2 (1901), 58–72, at 65, who thinks the *Didache* text the more original.

The way of death once again begins by picking up the second table of the Decalogue (*D* 5.1). We may note that there is a discernible relationship to the way of life, as the commandments prohibiting murder, adultery and theft are mentioned. We may compare the vice list, simply to note that the way of death is not the only such catalogue, with that found at Hermas, *Mandate* 8.3–5. "'Lord,' I said, 'what sorts of evil deed are they which we should keep ourselves from?' 'Listen,' he said. 'From adultery and fornication, from lawless drunkenness, from wicked greed, from too much food and extravagant wealth and boasting and hauteur and pride, and from lying and slander and hypocrisy, from bearing a grudge and from any blasphemy . . . '"[15]

Thus we may see that, once again, the tradition itself has been built up of other units; the way of death, or darkness, is the mirror of the way of life, or light.

The whole of the presentation of the two ways here must, however, be seen in context. The ideal of the humble and just person is stated in contradiction if not to the ways of the Graeco-Roman world then at least to Jewish views of that world. The Jew would look at the Hellenistic world and see depravity, idolatry and injustice in equal measure. It is from such a life that the (Jewish) Christians of the *Didache* community sought to rescue its converts, and in such a world that the material of the tradition continued to be presented.

---

[15]The whole of the eighth mandate, of which this is a very brief extract, is worthy of comparison with the TWT. Although it does not characterize two ways, and the vice list precedes the list of virtues (of which the first is faith and fear of the Lord) the whole is based, as is the two-ways section of the *Community Rule*, in a dualistic understanding of creation. There is certainly some common tradition here.

CHAPTER TWO

TWT in the second century

In this chapter we present three early Christian documents which incorporate the two ways as derived from the Jewish tradition. Because they are roughly contemporaneous, each deriving most probably from the second century, and cover much the same material, we also explore their inter-relationship for the insights which this gives us into the developing tradition.

PART ONE: THE DIDACHE

Introduction

The first Christian example of the two-ways teaching we present is the *Didache* (*D*). This document has variously been dated between 40 and 160 CE;[1] I am personally inclined to a date somewhere in the middle of this period, as I believe that in its present form it is the result of redactional activity, and that some time has to have passed during which this redactional activity occurred, though I would suggest that all the materials which constitute it are early indeed; the version of TWT, which is the focus of this book, has, as already suggested, undergone some editorial activity, but represents a version probably from late in the first century. This is not the place to argue over the process by which *D* was composed but we may observe that marks of redactional composition are patent; we may,

---

[1] See H. van de Sandt and D. Flusser, *The Didache: Its Jewish Sources and its Place in Early Judaism and Christianity* (Assen: Van Gorcum, 2002), 48–50.

for instance, note that the two versions of the eucharist in chapters nine and ten indicate some editorial development, and that the fourteenth chapter intervenes in a peculiar way in what would appear to be coherent instructions regarding the treatment of prophets. We may thus conclude that the document which we possess is at least the second edition, and that the editor used materials which existed independently. This is not, however, to deny that the finished work is a coherent whole with a definite purpose.

The two ways as found in *D* certainly had independent existence before its incorporation into *D*. In particular we may compare the presentation of the two ways of *D* to those found in three other documents, namely the Latin version of the two ways known as the *Doctrina apostolorum* (henceforth *L*) and to the version of the way of life found in the *Epitome of the teaching of the apostles* (*E*) and in the *Apostolic Church Order* (*K*), which documents are all introduced and translated further below. That the topics are presented in much the same order, as may be noted by comparing any of these to the two-ways sections of *The Epistle of Barnabas* (henceforth *B*) or of the *Community Rule*, makes it clear that there is a literary relationship. We explore this below, but note for the moment that much of the second chapter, which contains material similar to that found in St Matthew's Gospel, is unique to *D* and must therefore be the result of an editor's literary work. This is the section of *D* known as the "Gospel section." This may clearly be observed by looking at the synopsis of *D*, *L* and *B* at the end of this chapter. On the assumption that this block would not have been left out by subsequent editors we may initially suggest that *L* and *E/K* found the same block of material which is edited by *D*. Again, this is explored in more detail below, but the point to note is that *D* has edited the material quite independently of its original genesis.

This two-ways material is immediately followed by directions concerning baptism. There is, moreover, an explicit link made between the two ways and the following baptismal liturgy, in that the addressee, who is presumed to be the baptizer, is told firstly to rehearse the foregoing material. We may thus see that the *D* community employed the two ways as the instruction or training given for those coming to baptism in the community.

We may therefore suggest a setting in which *D* was, initially at least, put together. In doing so we may have reference to the suggestions of Slee, who notes the difficulties faced by early Jewish communities who, on confession of Christ, were faced with the issue of the admission of gentiles to the covenant and to define the circumstances under which table-fellowship might take place between Jew and gentile each of whom confessed Christ.[2] The issue was of particular significance because the central act of Christian worship is a meal. We read in Galatians of the dispute over table-fellowship between Jews and confessing gentiles in the context of a dispute between Paul and Peter.[3]

The parameters of the later Jewish debate may be observed in the Mishnah Tractate *Abodah Zarah*, which deals with idolatry, and thus with the extent to which Jews might relate to gentiles. A particular concern is that gentiles might pollute Jewish food with idolatrous practices, such as offering a part to an idol, and so food is forbidden unless it has been in continuous Jewish sight, such that no such offering might be made. "If an Israelite was eating with a gentile at a table and he put flagons on the table and flagons on the side-table and left the other there and went out, what is on the table is forbidden and what is on the side-table is permitted. If he had said to him "mix your cup and drink", that which is on the side-table is also forbidden also. Opened jars are forbidden . . ."[4] It is to be noted that, although set about by suspicion, the Jew and gentile are nonetheless at a common table. A more extreme view is represented in the Tosefta commentary on this Tractate: "R. Simeon b. Eleazar says 'Israelites who live abroad are idolaters. How so? A gentile who made

[2]Michelle Slee, *The Church in Antioch in the first century CE* (London: T&T Clark, 2003).

[3]Gal 2.11–16.

[4]M. *Abodah Zarah* 5.5.

a banquet for his son and went out and invited all the Jews who live in his town, even though they eat and drink their own (food and drink) and their own waiter stands over them and serves them, they nonetheless serve idolatry, as it is said "Lest you make a covenant with the inhabitants of the land and when they play the harlot after their gods and sacrifice to their gods and one invites you, you eat of his sacrifices."'" (Ex 34:15)[5]

This evidence is read by Slee as implying that gentile table-fellowship brought about impurity by its very nature and that any table-fellowship was thus impossible. However, as Sanders points out, ritual purity was necessary for Jews only in restricted circumstances (principally for service at the Temple), and thus Jews might well eat with gentiles without regard for the resulting ritual impurity.[6] Although we may suggest that eucharistic gathering might have required the same ritual purity as temple service, and thus that the presence of gentiles at the eucharistic gathering would generate a problem for believing Jews, noting that this is certainly the issue with which the fourteenth chapter of *D* deals, the two-ways material hardly deals with ritual matters at all. Beyond the avoidance of practices which might lead to idolatry, which in some later Jewish practice at least was sufficient to enable table fellowship to take place,[7] the purity which TWT demands is an ethical purity.

The particular danger in Slee's work is that she places all of this clearly at Antioch. Because of the peculiarity of the historical sources we are aware of issues at Antioch, in particular deriving from the presence of Paul there and his subsequent travels to other parts of the Empire, thus being provided with two sources for the early development of Christianity in the city, namely Acts and the Pauline letters themselves. But we need hardly be extending our imaginations overmuch by considering the possibility that the problems

[5]Tos. *Abodah Zarah* 4.6.

[6]E.P. Sanders "Jewish associations with gentiles and Galatians 2.11–14" in R.T. Fortna and B.R. Gaventa (eds.) *The conversation continues* (Nashville: Abingdon, 1990), 170–88.

[7]So BT *Gerim* 3.3.

faced in Antioch were far from unique, and that such issues came about wherever gentiles sought to join a Christian community of Israelite origin and culture; an understanding of the construction of *D* is thus not dependent on an Antiochene origin of the document. In other words, although *D* is not necessarily Antiochene, the incident at Antioch may be allowed to throw light upon the genesis of *D* by focusing our attention on table-fellowship and the necessity of integrating Jews and gentiles into a single community as the basis for *D's* genesis, and although *D* does not concern itself with ritual purity, and thus this is not the issue over which the division took place, the same is quite possibly true of the incident at Antioch. Thus if we knew the nature of the dispute at Antioch this may yet throw light on *D*.

Zetterholm notes that the description of the incident at Antioch in Galatians functions as the *narratio* of the letter, the initial narrative which sets the scene for any argumentative speech. There must, therefore, be some connection between this narrative and the argument which follows. The argument in Galatians, clearly, is about circumcision. Since circumcision was the means by which the covenant was demonstrated for male Jews, those males who are uncircumcised are therefore outside of the covenant of Israel. The same argument may well motivate the dispute to which Acts 15 makes reference. Zetterholm thus suggests that the argument concerned the manner in which Jews and gentiles might be members of a single group, of which commensality might be a sign; Jews had a covenantal relationship with God which gentiles might not enter except through becoming full proselytes, as a sign of which circumcision was considered essential. Although gentiles might be saved, they were not saved through that same covenant. If this is James' understanding, that of Paul is different, as he sees a single covenant for Jews and gentiles alike.[8] Although Zetterholm does not explore the extent to which this might impact on table-fellowship, disregard-

---

[8]Magnus Zetterholm, *The Formation of Christianity at Antioch* (London: Routledge, 2003), 129–166.

ing suggestions that the true issue was eucharistic fellowship, we may see that *D* makes no mention of Jew or gentile in fencing the table for the eucharistic meal, but anticipates that Jews and gentiles are gathered around a single table; they are each to participate in the body of Christ. We may suggest, therefore, that they are understood in Pauline terms to have entered a single covenant. As such, if the males are not to be circumcised and gentiles are not to become full proselytes, then some rite must be recognized as representing the single covenant into which the Jews and gentiles alike should be brought. This is baptism.

When, in later Judaism, a convert was made, instruction was given prior to circumcision and immersion:

> Our Rabbis taught: 'If at this time a man wants to become a proselyte, he must be asked: "What reason do have you for wanting to become a proselyte; do you not know that Israel at this time is afflicted and oppressed, despised, harassed and overcome by afflictions?" If he says, "I know and I am not worthy", he should be received immediately, and he should be taught in some of the lesser and some of the greater commandments. He should be taught about the sin [of the neglect of the commandments of] about gleanings, about the forgotten sheaf, the corner, and the tithe of the poor. He should be taught of the punishment for the transgression of the commandments. Furthermore, thus: "Be it known to you that before you came to this condition, if you had eaten suet you would not have been punished with *kareth,* if you had desecrated the Sabbath you would not have been punished with stoning; but now were you to eat suet you would be punished with *kareth;* were you to desecrate the Sabbath you would be punished with stoning." And just as he is told of the punishment for the transgression of the commandments, so is he informed of the reward granted for their fulfillment. He should be told, "Know that the world to come was made

only for the righteous, and all of Israel at this time is unable to accept either too much abundance, or too much retribution." He should not, however, be persuaded or dissuaded too much. If he accepted, he is circumcised right away.[9]

It is noted that women, by contradistinction to men, are simply immersed, but in their case likewise instruction is given. If we may see that baptism is being adopted as the means of constructing a covenant without circumcision then we may see **D** as presenting the two ways as the instruction which is to be given to gentiles who are to be so adopted into the covenant. By suggesting the two ways as providing a minimal standard for the behaviour of gentiles the editor of **D** is both establishing a fence around the community and ensuring that the territory so bounded is wide enough to include believing gentiles without insistence upon their adoption of the entirety of the Torah, and in particular in not insisting on male circumcision. In doing so a pattern of recognizable Jewish heritage is being adopted. The meal prayers of the ninth and tenth chapters likewise reflect a Jewish heritage through being modelled on Jewish table graces whilst at the same time delineating what is new in the confession of Christ, and indeed what is distinct about the Christian eucharist from any other Jewish meal.

The function of TWT in **D** therefore represents a radical breach in the Jewish tradition, even while the material included has a Jewish ancestry, by providing a means by which those who are not Israelites may nonetheless participate in the covenant.

At this point it may be objected that although it is reasonable to interpret the discussion between Peter and Paul at Antioch in covenantal terms, **D** makes no mention of covenant and that therefore, unless **D** is to be tied to this incident very closely, which we have refused to do, any such connection is void. However, this takes us to the very roots and genesis of the two ways. We have already observed several early Jewish uses of the two-ways tradition, including that

[9]BT *Yebamoth* 47A.

statement of Moses at Deuteronomy 30, at which point the law is being given. There is a significant allusion to this at Syriac Apocalypse of Baruch (2 Baruch) 19: "Therefore he appointed a covenant for them at that time and said: 'Behold, I appoint for you life and death,' and he called heaven and earth as a witness against them." The discourse on the two ways is understood here in clearly covenantal terms. One may also recall the covenantal context of the manner in which the *Community Rule* employed the TWT. Thus the very form of the two ways is itself covenantal, and recalls covenantal institutions to a Jewish audience. In this light the conditions imposed upon gentiles may be understood as constituting the basis for their admission to the Jewish covenant.

Even the form of the two ways may be a development from the covenantal form found in the Hebrew Bible. This has been formally analyzed as consisting of a salvation history, followed by stipulations to be followed by the parties to the covenant and then concluded with a statement of the blessings and curses which follow upon keeping, or failing to keep, the covenant.[10] This form is still visible not only in the *Testaments of the Twelve Patriarchs*, which have already been noted to have knowledge of the incipient two-ways tradition, but also in the *Community Rule*. The two ways in the *Community Rule* form the stipulations of the covenant, indeed the whole is described as being directed at Israel . . . "the community of the eternal covenant."

In this light, although *D* does not clearly demonstrate the covenantal form, in that an antecedent history is lacking, nonetheless we may suggest that at this point the association between TWT and the covenantal tradition was so well established that the formal apparatus for its transmission was no longer necessary. A hearer from a Jewish background would recognize the form of blessing and curse, commandment and prohibition, which is central to the Jewish identity as a people formed by covenant.

[10]Klaus Balzer, *The Covenant Formulary in Old Testament, Jewish and Early Christian Writings* (Oxford: Basil Blackwell, 1971).

We may conclude this discussion, therefore, in suggesting that the TWT in *D* is employed as a means by which gentiles might enter the covenant and participate, through baptism, in the community. Ideally they would take upon themselves the entirety of the law, but behaviour following the two ways, and abstention from food offered to idols, was sufficient.[11]

Translation

The instruction of the Lord to the gentiles through the twelve apostles

1 ₁There are two ways, the one of life and the one of death; the difference between the ways is great.

₂Now the way of life is this. First you shall love the God who made you, secondly your neighbour as yourself, and whatever you would not wish done to you, do not do to anyone else.

₃The instruction of these maxims is this: Bless those who curse you, and pray for your enemies, fast on behalf of those who persecute

---

[11]The reader should be warned that although the view of the *Didache* enunciated here is not eccentric or unique, it is not the only possible view. In particular Jonathan Draper argues that the *Didache* expects that the whole law should be kept by all, and that the behaviour prescribed by the two ways is a minimal standard to set gentiles on the way, but not the end of the process. His main argument that law is binding, rather than simply preferred, hinges on a passage in the final chapter, at which it is said that by the time of Christ's visitation the reader should have obtained that perfection. He links this to the suggestion in chapter 6, that the reader who desires to be perfect should keep the entire law. However, I believe that this is a relatively late part of the composition, and is secondary to the two ways, and that the author had not connected the two comments about perfection. The statement in chapter 16 is simply intended to combat lapse under trial, an exhortation similar to Barnabas 4.9. The perfection which the law is to bring about is perfection on earth, rather than eschatological perfection. For the contrary view see Draper's works "Torah and Troublesome Apostles in the Didache Community," *Novum Testamentum* 33 (1991), 347–372 and "A continuing enigma: The 'yoke of the Lord' in Didache 6:2–3 and early Jewish-Christian Relations," in P.J. Tomson and D. Lambers-Petry (eds), *The Image of Judaeo-Christians in Ancient Jewish and Christian Literature* (Tübingen: Mohr Siebeck, 2003), 106–123.

you. For what is the merit of loving those who love you? Do not even the gentiles do the same? But love those who hate you, and you shall have no enemy.

₄Abstain from fleshly and worldly lusts. If any one gives you a blow to your right cheek, turn the other to him also, and you will be perfect. If anyone obliges you to go a mile, go with him two; if anyone takes away your cloak, give him your coat also. If anyone takes what is yours from you, do not ask for it back, for you are unable.

₅Give to everyone who asks from you, and do not ask it back; for the Father wishes to give to all from his own graces. Whoever gives in accordance with the commandment is blessed, for he is free of guilt; but woe to anyone who receives. For anyone in need who receives is free of guilt; but anyone who receives when not in need shall stand trial as to why he received and for what purpose; and when in prison shall be examined concerning the things that he has done, and shall not depart thence until he has paid back the last cent.

₆But on this it was also said: "Let your alms sweat in your hands until you know to whom you are giving."

2   ₁The second commandment of the instruction: ₂You shall not murder, you shall not commit adultery, you shall not despoil a child, you shall not fornicate, you shall not steal, you shall not practise sorcery, you shall not make potions, you shall not murder a child through abortion nor kill it once born, you shall not covet what is your neighbour's, ₃you shall not swear falsely, you shall not bear false witness, you shall not speak evil, you shall not store up wrongs, ₄you shall not be double-minded or double-tongued. For being double-tongued is a snare of death. ₅Your word shall not be false, not empty, but shall be matched by action. ₆You shall not be grasping, nor rapacious, nor hypocritical, nor malicious, nor arrogant. You shall not plot evil against your neighbour. ₇You shall not hate any person, but some you shall rebuke, for some you shall pray, and some you shall love more than your own life.

3   ₁My child, shun every evil person and all who are like them. ₂Do not be quick-tempered, for anger leads to murder, nor jealous nor quarrelsome nor aggressive. For murder is begotten from these. ₃My child, do not be given over to passion, for lust leads to fornication, nor a speaker of base words, nor immodestly curious. For from all these adulteries are begotten.

₄My child, do not be an examiner of omens, since this leads to idolatry, nor an enchanter nor an astrologer nor a lustrator, nor desire to see[12] these things. For from all of these is idolatry begotten.

₅My child, do not be a liar, since falsehood leads to theft, nor a lover of money nor vainglorious. For from all of these are thefts begotten.

₆My child, do not be a grumbler, since it leads to blasphemy. Be not self-willed or evil-minded, for from all of these are blasphemies begotten.

₇Be generous, since the generous shall inherit the earth. (Ps 36.11) ₈Be patient, merciful, guileless and peaceable, good and fearing always the words which you heard. ₉You shall not make yourself haughty, nor give your life over to presumption. Do not spend your life with the exalted but associate with the righteous and lowly.

₁₀Whatever befall you, accept these experiences as good, knowing that nothing occurs without God.

4   ₁My child, you shall remember both night and day the one who speaks to you the word of God. You shall honour him as a master. For inasmuch as the dominion is discussed, the Lord is there. ₂You shall seek out daily the presence of the saints, that you may find refreshment in their words. ₃You shall not bring about schism, you shall reconcile those who are disputing, you shall judge justly, you shall not show partiality in rebuking any transgression. ₄You shall not be divided in your mind, whether it will be or not.

[12]Rordorf adds, from other versions of TWT "nor hear".

₅Do not be one who stretches out hands to take, whilst retracting them to avoid giving. ₆If you have possessions by means of your hands, you shall give a ransom for your sins. ₇You shall not hesitate about giving, nor shall you grumble when giving, for you know who is the good paymaster of rewards. ₈You shall not turn away a beggar. You shall share in common all things with your brother, and you shall not claim anything as your own. For if you are companions in immortality, are you not much more so in mortal matters?

₉You shall not withdraw your hand from your son or from your daughter, but from their youth you shall teach them the fear of God. ₁₀ You shall not command your servant or your maid, who put their hope in the same God, in bitterness, otherwise they may cease to fear the God who is set over both of you. For he does not make his call with regard to status, but with respect to those whom the spirit made ready. ₁₁You who are slaves shall be subject to your masters in reverence and fear as a representation of God.

You shall despise all hypocrisy, and everything that is not pleasing to the Lord.

You shall not forsake the commandments of the Lord. You shall preserve what you have received, neither adding nor subtracting. ₁₄You shall confess your transgressions in the assembly, and you shall not come to prayer with an evil conscience. This is the way of life.

5 ₁Yet the way of death is this.

First of all it is evil and beset by cursing. Murders, adulteries, lusts, fornications, thefts, idolatries, charms, sorceries, magic, robberies, falsities of witness, hypocrisies, double-heartedness, trickery, arrogance, malice, selfishness, greed, base speech, jealousy, insolence, haughtiness and pretence, ₂persecutors of the good, haters of the truth, lovers of falsity, unaware of the reward for righteousness, not associating with the good or with just judgement. Those who lie awake, not for good but for evil, far from generosity or patience, loving foolishness, pursuing a reward, showing no pity to the poor, doing no labour for the downtrodden, unaware of the one who made them, murderers of children, corrupters of what God has formed, turning away the needy, treading down the afflicted, advocates of the rich, lawless judges of the poor, utterly sinful. Children, may you be rescued from all of these.

6 ₁Beware lest anyone make you wander from this way of instruction, since they are instructing you apart from God.

₂If you are able to bear the entire yoke of the Lord you will be perfect. If you are unable, do what you can. ₃Now with regard to food, bear what you can, but keep strictly from what is offered to idols, for it is the worship of dead gods.

7 ₁Now with regard to baptism: baptize thus. When you have said all these things beforehand, baptize in the name of the Father and of the Son and of the Holy Spirit in living water. ₂If you have no living water baptize in another water, in warm, if you are unable (to do so) in cold. ₃If you have neither pour out water onto the head three times in the name of the Father and of the Son and of the Holy Spirit.

₄Now before baptism the one who baptizes should fast in advance, and the one being baptized, and others if they are able. You order the one being baptized to fast one or two days before.

8 ₁Your fasts should not be with the hypocrites for they fast on the fifth and the second of the week, yet you fast on the fourth and on the preparation (Friday). ₂Nor pray like the hypocrites, but as the Lord commanded in his Gospel:

Pray thus: Our Father in heaven, may your name be hallowed, may your Kingdom come, may your will come about as in heaven, so on earth. Our bread which is needed give us today. And relieve us of our debts as we also relieve those indebted to us.

And do not bring us into the trial but rescue us from the evil one.

Because the power and the glory are yours forever.

₃Pray in this way three times per day.

9 ₁Now with regard to the eucharist. You shall give thanks thus. ₂First, regarding the cup: "We thank you, our Father, for the holy vine of your servant David which you made known to us through your servant Jesus. Glory to you for ever."

₃So regarding the fragment: "We thank you, our Father, for the life and knowledge which you made known to us through your servant Jesus. Glory to you forever. ₄Just as this fragment was scattered over the mountains and, gathered together, became one, so may your church be gathered together from the ends of the earth into your Kingdom. Because the glory and the power is yours through Jesus Christ for ever."

₅Let nobody eat or drink from your eucharist but those baptized into the name of the Lord. For concerning this the Lord has said: "Do not give the holy to the dogs." (Cf. Mt 7.6)

10 ₁After you have been filled, give thanks thus. ₂"We thank you, holy Father, for your holy name which you caused to dwell in our hearts and for the knowledge and faith and immortality which you made known to us through your servant Jesus. Glory to you forever.

₃Almighty master, you created everything for the sake of your name. You gave both food and drink to people for their enjoyment so that they could give you thanks.

On us you bestowed spiritual food and drink and everlasting life through your servant. ₄Before all we thank you because you are powerful. Glory to you forever.

₅Remember your church, Lord, rescuing her from all evil, perfecting her in your love and gathering her together from the four winds, sanctified in your Kingdom which you prepared for her. Because the power and the glory are yours forever.

₆Let grace come and let this world pass away. Hosanna to the God of David.

Let anyone come who is holy. Let anyone who is not repent. Maranatha. Amen."

₇Allow the prophets to give thanks as much as they wish.[13]

11 ₁Receive anyone who instructs you in everything aforesaid. ₂But do not listen should any reverse their teaching and instruct you with other instruction, for destruction.

Receive anyone as a master if it is to supplement righteousness and knowledge of the Lord.

₃Now regarding apostles and prophets act thus, in accordance with the direction of the Gospel. ₄Every apostle who comes to you is to be received as a master, ₅who will not remain except a single day, a second if there is necessity. Anyone who remains three days is a false prophet.

₆On leaving you an apostle should take nothing except a single loaf, (to suffice) until further lodging is found. If any asks for money he is a false prophet.

₇Do not test any prophet speaking in the spirit; do not make discernment. Every sin is forgiven but this sin shall not be forgiven. ₈Not everyone speaking in the spirit is a prophet unless they are manifesting the conduct of the Lord. The false prophet and the prophet shall be known from conduct.

₉Every prophet ordering in the spirit that a table be set does not eat of it; otherwise he is a false prophet. ₁₀Every prophet teaching the truth yet not practising what is taught is a false prophet. ₁₁Every prophet who is tested and true, performing a worldly mystery of the church, yet not teaching you to do what he does shall not be judged of you, for he will have judgement with God. For so the ancient prophets acted.

[13]There is an additional section found here in the Coptic version, which also betrays its presence in the version of *D* presented in *Apostolic Constitutions*. Its originality and its meaning are both disputed. It reads: "Now concerning the word and the scent give thanks thus: 'We give thanks to you, Father, for the scent which you have made known to us through Jesus your child. Glory to you forever. Amen.'" It may be a reference to burning spices at a meal, to the scent of chrism at baptism or, as I firmly hold, a metaphorical reference to the scent of the wisdom of God. My argument may be followed in "The Word and the sweet scent: a rereading of the *stinoufi* prayer of the Coptic Didache" *Anaphora* 1 (2007), 53–64.

₁₂Do not listen should anyone say in the spirit "Give me money, or other things." Yet if he says you should give to others, who are in want, nobody should judge him.

12   ₁Everyone coming in the name of the Lord should be received; when you have tested him you shall know, for you shall have knowledge of right and left. ₂You should help, as much as you are able, anyone who comes to you as a traveller, who shall not remain with you except for two or three days, unless there is some constraint. ₃If he wishes to stay with you and has a trade he should work and eat. ₄If he has no trade, give some consideration beforehand so that you will know how a Christian should live among you without idleness. ₅If he does not wish to act in this way he is a Christ-tinker; beware of people like that!

13   ₁Every true prophet wishing to stay with you is worthy of his food. ₂Likewise a true teacher is worthy, as is a worker, of his food. ₃Thus you shall take every first-fruit of the winepress and the threshing floor, of your cattle and of your sheep, giving the first-fruit to the prophets for they are your high-priests. ₄If you have no prophet give them to the destitute. ₅If you make dough, take the first fruit, giving in accordance with the commandment. ₆Likewise take the first-fruit if you open a flask of oil or wine, giving to the prophets. ₇And of money and clothing and every possession, take the first-fruit as seems right to you, giving in accordance with the commandment.

14   ₁In accordance with the ‹commandment›[14] of the Lord, gather together to break bread and give thanks, first confessing your failings, so that your sacrifice may be pure. ₂Nobody who is in conflict with his companion should gather with you until they are reconciled so that your sacrifice is not defiled. ₃For this was said by the Lord: "'Offer me a pure sacrifice in every place and time because I am a

---

[14]There is no noun in the Greek version. Many translators take the word understood to be "day."

great King,' says the Lord, 'and my name is wonderful among the peoples.'" (Mal 1.11,14)

15 ₁Therefore appoint for yourselves overseers and agents worthy of the Lord, men who are generous and not money-loving and honest and tested, for they lend economic support to you for the service of prophets and teachers. ₂So do not look down on them for they are your honoured ones, together with the prophets and teachers.

₃Do not reprove one another in anger, but in peace, as you have it in the Gospel: Nobody should speak to anyone who harms another, nor should they hear from you, until he repent. ₄Perform your prayers and your charity and all you do as you have it in the gospel of the Lord.

16 ₁Be watchful of your life, do not let your lamps be quenched or your loins not girded, but be ready, for you do not know the hour at which Our Lord will come.

₂Gather together closely, seeking out whatever is fitting for your lives, for the whole period of your faith shall not profit you unless you have been perfected in the final time. ₃For in the last days false prophets and corrupters shall be multiplied, and sheep shall be turned into wolves and love shall turn into hate. ₄For as lawlessness increases they shall hate each other and persecute and betray. And then the deceiver of the world shall appear as a son of God, and shall perform signs and wonders, and the earth shall be betrayed into his hands. And he shall perform unlawful acts which have never occurred since the beginning of time. ₅Then shall the human creation come to the burning of testing, and many shall be trapped and destroyed, but those who have kept faith shall be saved by the very curse.[15] ₆And then the signs of truth shall appear, first the sign unrolled in heaven, then the sign of the trumpet's voice, and the

---

[15]There are three interpretations of the curse of which I am aware. My own conviction that the curse refers to Christ, the one who became accursed under the law.

third, the resurrection of the dead. ₇Yet not of all, but as was said: "The Lord will come and all his saints with him." ₈Then the world shall see the Lord coming upon the clouds of heaven.[16]

PART TWO: THE TEACHING OF THE APOSTLES (DOCTRINA APOSTOLORUM)

Introduction

The next Christian presentation of the two ways here is that known as the *Doctrina apostolorum*, preserved in Latin, though certainly a translation from Greek. It is hereafter abbreviated to *L*. This is a version of the two ways which, as may be observed by glancing at the synopsis, is close to *D*. However, it lacks the "Gospel section" and, like the *Community Rule* and, as we shall see, *B*, sets angels over the two ways.

It is extant in two mediaeval manuscripts, and would seem to have been in use in the mediaeval west as a version was in turn edited into a sermon attributed to Boniface. This sermon will be translated in chapter five.

According to van de Sandt and Flusser *L* represents a version of TWT more proximate to a Jewish original. They point to the absence

---

[16]This is the conclusion of *D* as found in the sole complete manuscript. However, it is possible that the copy from which this manuscript was in turn copied was defective and missed the last page, and that the *Apostolic Constitutions* reflects a more complete ending. The *Apostolic Constitutions* continues thus: ". . . with the power of his angels, and to recompense each in accordance with his conduct. Then shall the wicked go away into everlasting punishment, but the righteous shall go into life everlasting, inheriting those things which eye has not seen, nor ear heard, nor human heart conceived, which God has prepared for those who love Him; and they shall rejoice in the kingdom of God in Christ Jesus." We cannot know the extent to which *Apostolic Constitutions* reflects the precise wording of *D*, but may suggest that *D* went on from the appearance of The Lord to discuss the last judgement and the reward of the righteous. For such a view see R.E. Aldridge, "The Lost Ending of the Didache," *VC* 53 (1999), 1–15; for an alternative view see A. Milavec, *The Didache: Faith, Hope and Life of Early Christian Communities* (New York: Newman, 2003), 828–829, and 834–836.

of any specifically Christian material and the common presence of angelic intermediaries in *L* and in the *Community Rule*, as well as to small hints such as the words "in the world", used of the two ways, a phrase which is also to be found in the *Community Rule*,[17] as well as contrasting the conclusion to the concessive conclusion of *D*.[18] In general we must agree that *L* is closer in its thought world to the *Community Rule*, though whether this necessarily means it is "more Jewish" is a separate question; the question is open whether the redactor would have seen much in the way of a difference, that is to say, like Jesus, the redactor is Jewish and is working within a Jewish tradition even while the tradition is being extended and re-expressed.[19]

The proximity of the forms of TWT within *D* and *L* clearly indicates a literary relationship. There are three major differences between the two forms; the substantial addition to the tradition made by *D*, the concessive conclusion, and the absence of angelology.

Whereas it may readily be seen that the redactor of *D* might introduce material pertinent to his theme and so inserted the "Gospel section," the absence of the angelic intermediaries and the distinct conclusion are puzzling factors. With regard to the absence of angelic intermediaries Milavec makes a suggestion which is at least feasible, namely that *D* found reference to angels in the tradition but omitted it because gentile converts might be afraid of the consequences of offending those pagan gods who are recognized in *L* as angels of darkness. For *D* these pagan gods are simply dead, and the one God is the source and agency of all things.[20] However, we will note below that the opening of *D* is replicated in two third-century versions of TWT, namely *E* and *K* which also omit the *D* addition of the "Gospel section" and are thus unlikely to have derived directly

[17]Van de Sandt and Flusser, *Didache*, 62–63.

[18]Van de Sandt and Flusser, *Didache*, 120.

[19]A similar caution with regard to separating out Jewish and Christian strands in *D* is expressed by Milavec, *Didache*, 109–112.

[20]Milavec, *Didache*, 65.

from *D*. Thus Milavec's suggestion, whilst feasible, must be attributed not to *D* but to an earlier literary layer, which in turn makes it less likely. There are other possible explanations, namely that the redactor of *L* has re-introduced angelic mediators, or that, as Rordorf suggests, the tradition is diverse, and that there were versions like *D* which did not have a cosmologically dualist element and those which did.[21] With regard to the conclusion we may suggest the possibility that *L* has created an eschatological conclusion, on the basis of familiarity with the tradition from elsewhere, even while using as a literary basis a document shared with *D*, or indeed that the two ways in *D* originally had an eschatological conclusion, and that this is now found at chapter 16, having been separated from the two-ways material through the inclusion of additional matter.

If we agree that *L* is a version of TWT closely related to *D*, then the question is raised whether *D* is directly dependent upon *L* or whether the situation is more complex. In particular we must wrestle with Garrow's argument that, for all the apparently more primitive aspects, *L* is actually dependent upon *D*.[22] This is in contradiction to the majority opinion that *D* is derived from *L*.

As already noted, there are three major differences between the two, namely the presence of a block of material in *D* which is absent in *L* but which has parallels within the Gospels, apparently an insertion into the tradition, the absence of angelic intermediaries, and the distinct eschatological conclusion of *L*.

We have already suggested that *L* might have re-introduced angelic intermediaries into the tradition, and supplied an eschatological conclusion under the influence of a tradition of TWT proximate to the *Community Rule*, and so Garrow's suggestion is at first face to be preferred to a derivation of *D* from *L*, as otherwise the absence of the angelic intermediaries in *E* and *K* as well as the

[21]Willy Rordorf, "An Aspect of the Judeo-Christian Ethic: The Two Ways" in J.A. Draper, ed., *The* Didache *in Modern Research* (Leiden: Brill, 1996), 148–164, at 153.

[22]Alan Garrow, *The Gospel of Matthew's Dependence on the* Didache (London: T&T Clark, 2004), 68–75.

absence of the Gospel section would be hard to explain. However, the essence of Garrow's argument lies in the nature of the introduction of the Gospel material in **D**:

> The instruction of these maxims is this . . .

He notes that the same introduction is found in **L**, in which case it goes on to cover not the Gospel material but the material which is found in **D**.2. In **D** this other material is introduced by a further introduction:

> The second commandment of the instruction is this . . .

If **D** is dependent upon **L** then one must assume that **D** employed the first introduction already extant to introduce the new material and then constructed a new heading to introduce the traditional material. Garrow suggests that this is strange behaviour, and that one would expect the new material to be introduced with the new heading, and the old material to retain its existing heading. The other point is that the significance of stating that this is the "second commandment" is unclear. "Does the interpolation interpret the first commandment while 2.2–7 expands the second, or is it a primary interpretation of the second commandment, while 2.2–7 is a secondary one?"[23] He suggests therefore that the interpolation is actually the first introduction. Thus, according to Garrow, the statement "the second commandment of the teaching" stood in the original, and made complete sense as interpreting the second part of the love commandment.

This suggestion, however, introduces problems of it own. Firstly we must assume that **L** omitted not only the "interpolated" material but also the second introduction (quite apart from omitting the rest of **D**!). According to Garrow **L** is doing this not because he is attempting to make TWT more "primitive" but because he is

[23]Garrow, *Dependence*, 69.

creating something useful for the instruction of catechumens. But why then should he omit, several times, the address to "my child"? Fundamental, however is the problem of the dual introduction. Why, we must ask, is *D* content to introduce new material with an old introduction?

The answer, we must suggest, is that it is precisely because it is new material that the old introduction is employed. New material is being employed as old, and the new insights of the Christian tradition are being introduced as though they were the old and wedded to the pre-Christian origins of the tradition. "Second" therefore, as an introduction to the commandments of the decalogue, is used in the sense of "secondary", since the new material is seen to take precedence over the old, as the law is interpreted through Christ.

This does not, however, necessarily mean that *D* is dependent directly upon *L*, even though we suggest that *D* had interpolated the tradition and that *L* is a version closer to the roots of TWT. For Garrow observes other, albeit minor, problems with such a theory. One such is the appearance of a line found in *D*'s interpolation within *L*, though in a different context. *D* 1.5a appears at *L* 4.8. Niederwimmer's explanation is that *D* omitted the line here to avoid repetition, but Garrow is quick to note that *D* is not afraid of repetition elsewhere, and suggests that *L* took the line from *D* because it fitted his purpose at this point.

Is it not possible, however, that this is a piece of free-floating tradition which was employed independently by *D* and *L* and placed in a section which is most germane? However, if this is the case then there is no mutual direct dependence of *D* and *L* upon each other. Other small points, quite apart from the problem posed by the introductions of *E* and *K* already mentioned, speak against such dependence, for instance the failure of *L* to mirror *D*'s prohibition on stealing, the minor differences in the order in which prohibitions and commands are found, the omission of *D* 3.3–4a by *L*, and the very distinct conclusions. Balzer indeed notes that these conclusions point to the greater proximity of *L* than *D* to the tradition, since, like the *Community Rule* and other representatives of the covenantal formulary, there is clearly here a blessing and a curse set forth upon those who keep or do not keep the teaching.[24]

I suggest that rather than being in a direct literary relationship *D* and *L* are in indirect literary relationship. In other work I suggest that there was a branch of TWT which organized the material much as did *D*, though lacking *D*'s interpolation. This I termed δ, seeing it as the predecessor of *D* in the redactional chain. I may now build on this hypothesis by suggesting that *L* is likewise a derivative of δ. There is a limit to the extent to which δ may be reconstructed, and in particular its conclusion cannot be known. It may be eschatological, in which case it is preserved by *L*, or may be concessive, in which case it is preserved by *D*, or may be neither as *D*'s concessive conclusion and *L*'s eschatological conclusion can, with equal ease, be attributed to these documents' respective redactional interests.

However, quite apart from the existence of *L*, it is the appearance in later centuries of versions of the TWT organizing the material much as does *D* but omitting the "Gospel section" which makes the existence of a δ branch of the tradition more than probable.

Thus, in constructing a diagram of relationships a start may be made thus:

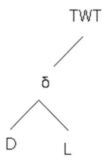

Before proceeding further in our construction of the history of the tradition there is a third early manifestation of TWT which is clearly distinct from *L* and *D*. We deal with this after presenting the text of *L*.

Translation

Teaching of the Apostles

1   ₁There are two ways in the world, of life and death, of light and darkness. Two angels are set over them, the one of justice, the other of wickedness. For the difference between the two ways is great.

₂Now the way of life is this. First you shall love the eternal God who made you, secondly your neighbour as yourself. Whatever you would not wish done to you, do not do to anyone else.

₃The meaning of these maxims is this:

2   ₂You shall not commit adultery, you shall not murder, you shall not bear false witness, you shall not despoil a child, you shall not fornicate, you shall not practise sorcery, you shall not make potions, you shall not destroy a child through abortion nor kill it once born, you shall not covet what is your neighbour's. ₃You shall not swear falsely. You shall not speak evil, you shall not store up wrongs, ₄you shall not be double-minded in giving, nor double-tongued. For the tongue is a snare of death.

₅Your word shall not be empty, nor false. ₆You shall not be greedy nor grasping, nor rapacious, nor hypocritical, nor arrogant nor malicious. You shall not plot evil against your neighbour. ₇You shall not hate any person, some you shall love more than your own life.

3   ₁Child, shun the evil person, and a person who is like to him. ₂Do not be quick-tempered, for anger leads to murder, nor quarrelsome or aggressive. For anger is begotten from all of these. ₄Do not be an astrologer, nor a lustrator, these things lead to empty superstition. Nor desire to see or hear. ₅Do not be a liar, since falsehood leads to theft, nor a lover of money nor vain glory. From all of these are thefts begotten. ₆Do not be a grumbler, since it leads to blasphemy. Do not be self-willed or evil-minded. For from all of these are blasphemies begotten. ₇Be generous, since the generous will possess the sacred earth. ₈Be patient in difficulty, good and fearing all the words which you hear. ₉You shall not make yourself haughty, nor make yourself honourable among people, nor give your life over to presumption. Do not spend your life with the exalted but associate with the righteous and lowly.

₁₀Whatever mishaps befall you, accept these experiences as good, knowing that nothing occurs without God.

4 ₁You shall remember day and night the one who speaks to you the word of the Lord God, You shall honour him as a master. Whence what is of the Lord proceeds, the Lord is there.

₂Seek out the presence of the saints, that you may find refreshment in their words.

₃You shall not bring about schism, reconcile those who are disputing, judge justly, knowing that you will be judged. You shall not defraud anyone in his business.

₄You shall not be doubtful whether it will be or not.

₅Do not be one who stretches out a hand to take whilst retracting to avoid giving back. ₆If you have gained by means of your hands a ransom for your sins, ₇you shall not hesitate about giving nor shall you grumble when giving, for you know who is the good paymaster of this reward. ₈You shall not turn your back upon a beggar. You shall share in common all things with your brothers, and you shall not claim anything as your own. For if we are companions in immortality, how much more should we go on from there. For the Lord desires that we should give to all out of his gifts.

₉You shall not withdraw your hand from your children, but from their youth you shall teach them the fear of the Lord.

₁₀You shall not command your servant or your maid in rage; they put their hope in the same God. He should fear both God and you. For he does not make his call with regard to status, but those in whom he finds the spirit. ₁₁You who are slaves are to be subject to your masters in reverence and fear as a representation of God.

₁₂You shall despise all hypocrisy and you shall not do what is not pleasing to God.

₁₃Child, preserve what you have heard, neither adding what is contrary to them, nor subtracting.

₁₄You shall not come to prayer with an evil conscience.

This is the way of life.

5   ₁For the way of death is opposed to it.

Firstly it is evil and beset by cursing, adulteries, murders, falsities of witness, fornications, wrongful lusts, sorceries, wicked potions, thefts, vain superstitions, grasping, hypocrisies, contempt, malice, insolence, greed, base speech, jealousy, insolence, haughtiness and pretence, ₂not fearing, persecutors of the good, haters of the truth, lovers of falsity, those unaware of the reward of veracity, not associating with the good or with just judgement. Those who lie awake, not for good but for evil, far from generosity and close to pride, pursuing a reward, showing no pity to the poor, not mourning for those who mourn, unaware of the one who made them, murderers of their children, abortionists, turning away from good works, depriving the labourer, advocates of those who rob the just. Child, keep yourself from all of these.

6   And beware lest anyone make you wander from this instruction, since they are instructing you apart from the teaching. ₄If you act thus habitually and daily you shall be close to the living God. But if you do not do it you shall be far from the truth. ₅Keep all this in your mind and do not be deceived with regard to your hope, but you shall come to the crown through these sacred struggles. ₆Through our Lord Jesus Christ, reigning and governing with God the Father and the Holy Spirit for ever and ever.

Part three: The Epistle of Barnabas

Introduction

The third early Christian presentation of the TWT which we present is the *Epistle of Barnabas* (henceforth ***B***). Not much is certain about this letter, and anything that is known has to be gleaned from internal clues. The consensus supports an Alexandrian provenance;[25] in support of this we may certainly agree that a scholastic form of Christianity such as that which obtained in some Alexandrian circles, gave rise to the letter, as there are many elements which mark a schoolroom style, such as frequent indications of an audience, with exhortations to learn, to listen and to understand. Likewise the letters engagement with Judaism is consistent with an Alexandrian provenance. Our concern, however, is less with provenance than with the use the letter makes of TWT.

The TWT section of ***B*** appears at the end of the document. The thrust of the major part of the letter is to interpret various provisions of Jewish law in a spiritual direction, with the intention of showing that these institutions are no longer valid, whilst at the same time preserving a place in the church for what in time would be the Old Testament. We may well see this re-reading of the Hebrew Bible as responding to other strands within Judaism, and particular as responding both to nationalistic attempts to restore the Temple and to the emergence of rabbinic Judaism with its own all-encompassing reading of the law. We must see how TWT relates to those agenda.

If we compare the TWT in ***B*** to that presented in ***D*** and ***L*** the following features emerge:

1) There is material in ***D*** which does not appear in ***L*** or ***B***.

---

[25] See most recently J. Loman, "The Letter of Barnabas in early second-century Egypt," in A. Hilhorst and G.H. van Kooten, eds., *The Wisdom of Egypt: Jewish, Early Christian and Gnostic Essays in Honour of Gerard P. Luttikhuizen* (Leiden: Brill, 2005), 247–265.

This is the material which was identified as *D*'s insertion into the tradition, the Gospel section. Its absence in *B* tends to confirm the conclusion that *D* had inserted it into the δ tradition.

2) There is material in *D* and *L* which does not appear in *B*.

Chiefly this is the material found addressed to "my child." This would imply that this material was itself a block which had been inserted into the tradition, and marks off the δ branch of the network of TWT as distinct through the inclusion of this material. Beyond that, moreover, the double love commandment is also missing from *B*.

3) The order of the presentation of the material in the way of life in *B* is distinct from that of *D* and *L*. *D* and *L*, whatever their other divergences, contain substantially the same material arranged in the same order. Whereas there is a significant overlap in contents, *B* is quite distinct for the most part in the order in which the material is presented.

The implication of this is that *B* is

i: a deliberate re-arrangement of the TWT as received by *D* (and *L*) from the δ tradition, or

ii: the form of TWT as received by the δ tradition which δ had reordered, or

iii: a different and independent form of TWT.

We consider each of these possibilities in turn.

That *B* is a reordering of *D* was suggested by Goodspeed, and has received recent support from van de Sandt and Flusser, as well as being cautiously suggested by Draper.[26]

Goodspeed's argument centres on seeing *B* as an improvement on *D*. In observing the omission of material in *B* he suggests:

[26]E.J. Goodspeed, "The Didache, Barnabas and the Doctrina," *Anglican Theological Review* 27 (1945), 228–247;van de Sandt and Flusser, *Didache*, 60–61; J.A. Draper, "Barnabas and the Riddle of the Didache Revisited," *JSNT* 58 (1995), 89–113.

> ... a closer examination of Barnabas' great omission ...
> shows that much of it—murder, lust, enchantment, magic,
> lying, avarice, grumbling,—are covered elsewhere in Barn-
> abas ... mostly in *positive* command, adjusted to a loftier
> plane of Christian living. . . . Anger, murder, enchantment,
> magic and grumbling are covered either generally or spe-
> cifically in Barn 19:3–11. It is a mistake to suppose Didache
> superior to Barnabas in its presentation of the Two-Ways
> material; Didache is in fact inferior, for it contains some
> repetitions which Barnabas strips off . . . Moreover Barnabas
> presents not so much vices to be shunned as virtues to be
> cultivated . . . The average Christian then as now does not so
> much need to be told not to murder . . . as to be kind, gener-
> ous, pure and true.[27]

Attractive as this argument is, it does not really hold up. If this is
B's plan it not consistently applied, for not only does *B* positively
assert that Christians are not to fornicate, which one might suggest
that Christians do not need to be told not to do any more than they
should be told not to murder, but many of the *D* passages which do
not appear in *B* are warnings that lesser foibles may turn to greater
sins.

Whereas Goodspeed's argument is based on seeing *B* as an
improvement on *D*, the argument of van de Sandt and Flusser
derives from a view of *B* as inferior! Their argument is the essentially
negative one that it is hard to imagine how the ordered form of *D*
(and *L*) might emerge from *B*. *B* is "chaotic", and so the ordered form
of paraenesis in *D* can hardly have been created by unravelling the
form in *B*.[28] In answer we might say that, if *D* is such a reasonable
and rational presentation, it is even harder to see why *B* should wish
to confuse it.

---

[27]Goodspeed, "The Didache, Barnabas and the Doctrina," 235–236.
[28]Van de Sandt and Flusser, *Didache*, 60.

Something of an answer to this is offered by Draper, who suggests that *B* is a hostile witness to *D*, and that *B* is an ironic presentation of the catechetical material of the *D* community. *D* is essentially still Jewish Christian, whereas *B* is virulently anti-Jewish.[29] Even if this were demonstrable, it would explain only why the TWT is relegated to an appendix in *B*, but would not explain the distinct order of presentation. If the suggestion above that *D*'s presentation of TWT is undertaken precisely in order to admit gentiles to the community without law-obedience, then Draper's conclusion is all the harder to sustain. For on this understanding, although *D* derives from a Jewish tradition and numbers Jews among its believers, it is radically distinct from the form of Jewish Christianity in its attitude to gentiles espoused by, for instance, James. Finally, as we note below, there are some parallels between TWT material and content within the main body of *B*. It would be odd, were *B*'s concern to contradict or redefine TWT in some way, to find support for precepts within TWT within the main body of the text.

However, an interesting point in Draper's study, which will prove pertinent to the use of TWT by *K*, is the suggestion that TWT is transformed by *B* from a baptismal catechesis to advanced teaching. That *D* uses TWT in a manner which conforms to its original generation, in which it is found in the *Community Rule*, is confirmed, as we have already seen, by the instruction to baptize following the presentation of TWT, but *B* presents this teaching as for the advanced. To an extent it might be suggested that literary documents present material only to those who are literate and, moreover, that even *D* is addressed to those who are advanced, in that it is addressed to those who are to undertake the baptism of those who are catechized using TWT. But it remains the case that this material, albeit mediated, is addressed to catechumens, whereas *B* presents this material as additional to the substantive teaching which has already been given. So, in comparison to *K*, which has a similar eschatological conclusion to that in B, we may note that there is a difference in the

[29]Draper, "Barnabas and the Riddle of the Didache," 89–113.

address of the eschatological conclusion which in **K** is addressed to "brothers" but in **B** is addressed to those in positions of leadership. This is a clear indication that **B** has removed the material from its catechetical frame, as Draper suggested. But there is no proof here that **B** reorders **D** as, even if there is a relationship, the reordering of the material is not what distinguishes the uses to which it is put and there is no reason on this basis to undertake a re-ordering.

Critical for anyone wishing to argue for **B** as a rearrangement of **D** is the "great omission" to which Goodspeed refers, that is to say the absence of the material addressed to "my child." We have already suggested that this material was added at an earlier level of redaction, namely the common root of **D** and **L** which we have termed δ.[30] This means that, unless we were to postulate an even earlier version of δ, then we cannot know that the order found by **B** was anything like **D**. It may well derive from an entirely independent part of the tradition, which we may term β. Van de Sandt and Flusser by contrast suggest that it is equally possible that **B** omitted the block;[31] this would in turn imply that the block was established as a block prior to δ in TWT, and requires anyone wishing to argue that **B** rearranged TWT material found in an order proximate to that of **D** to explain the rearrangement as a whole, including the deliberate omission of this block. In any event it is hard to justify seeing **B** as a rearrangement of **D**.

The contrasting view, that **D** is a re-ordering of **B** was extensively argued in the twentieth century, but these arguments largely derived from the rather eccentric view that **D** was a late fiction, intended to create a primitive past to the apostolic church.[32] If, as we have

[30]Niederwimmer, *Didache*, 63; R.A. Kraft, *The Apostolic Fathers 3: Barnabas and the Didache* (New York: Nelson, 1965), 146.

[31]Van de Sandt and Flusser, *Didache*, 73–74. In view of the linkage between these sayings and Jewish tradition observed by Kraft, *Apostolic Fathers*, 146, it is more likely than not that this material was part of TWT before its Christian adoption. Kraft, however, believes that the material was joined to the tradition before the β branch diverged.

[32]The classic statement is that of J.A. Robinson, *Barnabas, Hermas and the Didache* (London: SPCK, 1920).

already suggested, *D* is dependent upon an earlier form of TWT, then the suggestion becomes yet more convoluted, as it would have to have been the earlier form which re-ordered *B*.

We are thus left with the third possibility, that *B* is indeed an independent strand in TWT. Let us sum up what has already been suggested.

At the earliest stage lies a loose collection of material employed by various groups within forming Judaism. We have seen that this traditional material enters Christian usage, and in one form is a source for *D* and *L*, with the addition of material, namely the sayings addressed to "my child" and the double love commandment. However, it is clearly present in a separate form in *B*. There are some similarities, and the section on the negative way is particularly close. *B* moreover has retained the angelology which is a mark of a similar origin, though it refers to the ways as ways of light and darkness rather than of life and death (so *D*). *L*, interestingly, uses both terms. We may thus suggest that at a stage earlier than δ, the version of TWT found in *B* had branched off from TWT.

This does not mean that the extant *B* is earlier than *D*, simply that it has access to a version of the tradition which precedes the δ branch. We may, moreover, accept this without commitment to any particular rationale for the difference in shape between *B* and δ. We may, however, particularly note the cosmological dualism and the statement that angels are set over the ways, which makes this branch of the tradition closer to that of the *Community Rule* than the δ branch.

Nonetheless, the study has alerted us to the distinct use of TWT in *B* and *D*. Whereas *D* clearly preserves the function of TWT in catechesis, this is not the case in *B*. Niederwimmer therefore questions the common characterization of TWT as catechetical, suggesting instead (following Wengst), a school-setting.[33] This may be the setting for *B*, but *B* may, as Draper suggests, have altered the context

[33]Niederwimmer, *Didache*, 37–38.

of TWT through the inclusion of this traditional material into his discourse, and in particular by including it as an appendix.

The incorporation of traditional material is largely the manner in which *B* has been constructed overall. It is possible that *B* is no more than a compilation, in which case TWT is simply another element in the relatively unordered compilation. However, Carleton Paget, in studying the central chapters, has argued that the redactor has put his own stamp on the material which he has received.[34] Since the TWT material in *B* is probably not a re-arrangement of the δ tradition we cannot perceive a particular interest in the order of presentation, but may be alert to a particular agendum in the inclusion and the presentation of the material.

There is nothing in the content which is contradictory to what stands before. Thus at 2.7, *B* cites Zechariah 8.17: "None of you should harbour evil against a neighbour in your heart, nor should you love a false oath." The thought, if not the expression, is close to TWT. Further below, at 4.2, *B* states that the dark one should not insinuate himself into the Christians' community and that we should therefore shun the deeds of the "wicked way." Once again the TWT is echoed. Again, at 5.4, *B* states, in terminology reminiscent of his presentation of TWT, ". . . a person is who has insight into the way of righteousness but remains on the way of darkness is deservedly destroyed." (5.4) After some general reflections the epistle comes to deal with the specific issues relating to Judaism which are at the heart of its message, namely food laws, circumcision, the Sabbath and the temple. Here, likewise, there are points made analogous to those made within TWT, for instance in the tenth chapter there are warnings about associating with the wicked, an interpretation of the ban on eating the hare as a warning against the corruption of children and of the ban on eating the hyena as a warning against adultery. This is not to state that this teaching is received from the TWT but

---

[34]James Carleton Paget, *The Epistle of Barnabas: Outlook and Background* (WUNT 2.64; Tübingen: Mohr-Siebeck, 1994).

simply to point out that what is said is entirely in conformity with the content of the tradition.

Is it too much to suspect that in spite of its appearance as an appendix the presentation of TWT is central to *B*'s purpose? Like the other material within the letter it is mediated through a school tradition, as Wengst rightly notes; we may, moreover, observe the statement that TWT is being presented as a further instruction and information in the light of Barnabas' opening statement that his purpose is to impart information, and that this information is intended to supplement the existing faith of the audience. May we therefore suggest that the author is imparting an ethical lesson to accompany the spiritual interpretation of the law which the major part of the letter has promulgated, propounding TWT in particular as a substitute for the ethical content of the law which might otherwise be spiritually interpreted and disregarded? We may, moreover, recall our earlier discussion of TWT and covenant, in which it was argued that TWT formally functioned as part of the covenantal relationship established by baptism in *D*. Yet *B* argues that the Jews never received the covenant, that the only covenant is that made with Christians. If Christians are seen as a covenantal people some stipulations are needed by which they are to remain within the covenant; these stipulations are provided by the inclusion of TWT within the teaching. Moreover, as Balzer, who likewise discerns a covenantal form behind *B*, though perhaps exaggerating the case in seeing the major part of the document as an "antecedent history," points out, these ethical stipulations are concluded by a blessing on those who keep them and a curse on those who do not, in conformity with covenantal models.[35] Thus while not accepting Balzer's argument that the whole of *B* is modelled on a covenant, the TWT appendix, I suggest, is derived from precisely such a model.

In this brief discussion we have concluded that *B* represents a strand in TWT which is distinct from δ. Thus it is likely that this version represents the original thought that the hearer should remem-

[35]Balzer, *Covenant Formulary*, 125–127.

ber the day of judgement, rather than remembering his teacher, and that the change is the work of the δ redactor. We have also concluded that in spite of the appearance of the two-ways material in an appendix, the content is close to Barnabas' overall intention.

In the light of this discussion we may conclude by supplementing the diagram found earlier, before giving the text.

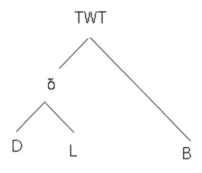

Translation

The Letter of Barnabas

1 ₁Greetings, sons and daughters, in the name of the Lord who loved us, in peace.

₂The richness and wealth of God's acts of goodness towards you are such that I rejoice immeasurably in your blessed and glorious spirits, so much have you received the grace of the spiritual gift planted in you. ₃Thus I rejoice all the more with you within myself in the hope of salvation, since among you I surely see the spirit pouring forth upon you from the wealth of the spring of the Lord. So struck am I that I long to see you face to face. ₄I am aware that I have spoken much to you, because I know that the Lord has accompanied me on the way of righteousness, and so I am persuaded, and indeed am compelled, to love you more than my own life, for a great hope and love dwell among you in hoping for his life. ₅Reasoning that if I had sufficient concern for you as to hand over a portion from what I have received I should receive a reward, I hasten to send to you briefly, so that you might have perfect insight to accompany your faith.

₆For there are three teachings of the Lord of life.

Hope, the beginning and end of our faith,

And righteousness, the beginning and end of judgement.

Love, bearing witness to our gladness and rejoicing at what is done in righteousness.

₇For the master has made known to us through the prophets what occurred, and what is happening now, and what is to be, giving us the first-fruits as a taste. As we see that everything is coming about just as he said it would be we should make offering more abundantly and more exaltedly in awe of him. ₈Whereas I, not as a teacher but as one of yourselves, shall demonstrate a few things to you, through which you may rejoice in what is now occurring.

2   ₁As the days are evil and the one who works thus is presently in power, we should set ourselves to seek out the righteous deeds of the Lord. ₂Awe and endurance are assistants to our faith, patience and self-control do battle alongside us. ₃While these remain holy to the Lord, wisdom, understanding, perception and insight rejoice in their company. ₄For he has clearly shown through all the prophets that he has no need of sacrifices or holocausts or offerings when he says: ₅" 'What is the volume of your sacrifices to me,' says the Lord. 'I am full of your holocausts of rams, and I do not want the fat of lambs and the blood of bulls and goats, not even when you come to appear before me. Who has besought these things from your hands? Do not continue to walk in my courts! If you bring me fine flour it is point-less, incense is loathsome to me. I cannot abide your new moons and your Sabbaths.' " (Is 1.11–13) ₆He cancelled all of this so that the new law of our Lord Jesus Christ, which is without the yoke of compulsion, should provide an offering not of human making. ₇And again he says to them: "Did I command your ancestors, on coming out of the land of Egypt, to offer me holocausts and sacrifices? (Jer 7.22) ₈But rather I commanded this of them, 'None of you should harbour evil against a neighbour in your heart, nor should you love a false oath.'" (Zech 8.17) ₉We ought therefore to perceive our Father's knowledge of what is good, since we are not ignorant, because he is speaking to us, wishing us not to be deceived as they were, desiring us to seek how we might make offering to him. ₁₀Therefore he speaks to us thus: "A sacrifice to the Lord is a humbled heart, a scent of sweetness to the Lord is a heart which glorifies the one who made it." (Ps 50[51].19) And so, brothers, we should learn more carefully about our salvation, so that the evil one may not throw us far from our life through smuggling error in.

3 ₁So again he speaks about this to them: "'Why do you fast for me,' says the Lord,' so that your voice may be heard crying out today? I have not chosen this fast,' says the Lord, 'not a person abasing his soul. ₂Even should you bow your neck into a circle and put on sack-cloth and lie down[36] on ashes you should not call this an acceptable fast.'" (Is 58.3–5) ₃He says to us: "'Look, this is the fast which I have chosen,' says the Lord. 'Loosen every bond of injustice, release the compulsion of forced agreements, send forth the downtrodden in freedom, and tear up every unjust contract. Share your bread with the hungry, and clothe anyone naked you might see. Invite those living rough into your home, and do not, either you or anyone from your children's households, despise anyone you might see who has been humbled. ₄Then like the dawn will your light burst forth, and you shall quickly gird up your clothing, righteousness will go before you and the glory of God shall surround you. ₅Then you will cry out and God will hear you,—even while you are speaking he shall say "Look, I am here," if you retreat from your bondage and the scornful gesture and the word of grumbling and give bread to the hungry from your heart and take pity on the humbled one.'" (Is 58.6–10) ₆For this purpose, brothers, did the one who is patient reveal to us about

[36]Perhaps "lie down" should be omitted, in accordance with some MSS.

all this beforehand, foreseeing that the people he prepared in his beloved one would believe, so that we would not be dashed against that law of theirs.

4 ₁We should discover what is able to save us as we carefully explore what is occurring now. Let us flee absolutely all deeds of lawlessness so that works of lawlessness do not overwhelm us. And we should despise the error of the present time so that we may be loved in that which is to come. ₂Let us give no respite to our souls, allowing them to form alliances with the wicked and with sinners, lest they be conformed to them. ₃The final stumbling block has drawn near, about which it has been written, as Enoch says. For this reason the master truncated the times and the days, so that his beloved might make haste and come to his inheritance. ₄Thus the prophet also says: "Ten kingdoms shall reign upon the earth and afterwards a small king shall arise who will humble three of the kings at the same time." (Dan 7.24) ₅Similarly Daniel speaks of him: "And I saw the fourth beast, wicked and strong and more dangerous than all the beasts of the sea, and as ten horns arose from him, a small horn grew out from them and humbled three of the large horns at once." (Dan 7.7–8) ₆You should understand.

I am asking this as one of yourselves, simply as one who loves you all more than myself, take care of yourselves and do not be conformed to those who heap up your sins and say that their covenant remains ours. ₇It is ours, but they lost it even as Moses was receiving it! ₈For Scripture says: "Moses was fasting on the mountain for forty days and forty nights and received the covenant from the Lord written on stone tablets by the finger of the hand of the Lord." (Ex 31.18; 24.28) But when they turned to idols they lost it. For the Lord speaks thus: "Moses, Moses, come down quickly, for your people, whom you brought out of Egypt, are lawless." (Ex 32.7) Moses understood and threw the two tablets from his hands and their covenant was broken so that that of the well-beloved Jesus might be branded onto our hearts in our hope in his fidelity. ₉I wish to write a great deal, not as a teacher but in a manner befitting one who loves, and I am keen to write, as your devoted slave, not leaving out anything that we possess. So let us pay attention in the last days, for the entire period of our fidelity will count for nothing unless now, in this period of lawlessness, we also take a stand against the stumbling blocks which are imminent, as befits children of God, $_{10}$so that the dark one should not slip in among us. Let us flee all foolishness and despise utterly the works of the wicked way. Do not withdraw by yourselves as though you were already made just but come together for a common purpose and seek out the common good $_{11}$for Scripture says: "Woe to those who have understanding in themselves and are knowledgeable in their own sight." (Is 51.21) Let us be spiritual, let us be a perfect temple to God. As far as it is within us let us cultivate the fear of God and struggle to keep his commandments so that we may rejoice in his righteous demands.

$_{12}$The Lord will judge the world without respect of persons; each will receive in accordance with what he did. If good his justice shall precede him, if wicked before him shall be the reward of wickedness, $_{13}$so that as those who are called we should never lie down in forgetfulness of our sins, allowing the wicked one to govern and take authority against us to force us out of the Kingdom of the Lord. $_{14}$Think on this, now, my brothers, when you see such signs and wonders which occurred in Israel. And yet still it is abandoned. We should pay close attention, as it is written, "Many are called yet few are found chosen." (Mt 22.14)

5 $_1$It was in order that we might be cleansed by the forgiveness of our sins, which is in the sprinkling of his blood, that the Lord allowed his flesh to be given over to corruption. $_2$Some of those things which are written about him are addressed to Israel, others to us. It states this: "He was wounded through our lawlessness and he was abused through our sins. We are healed through his bruising. As a sheep he was led to slaughter and like a lamb silent before the shearer." (Is 53.5,7)

₃Therefore we should give thanks all the more to the Lord, because he has revealed to us what has passed, and has made us wise in what is now occurring and we are not without understanding of what is to be. ₄Scripture says: "It is not unjust that nets are spread out for the birds." (Prov 1.17) That means that a person who has insight into the way of righteousness but remains on the way of darkness is deservedly destroyed.

₅Now think of this, my brothers: If the Lord, the Lord of all the world, to whom God at the creation of the world said "Let us make humanity after our image and likeness," (Gen 1.26) allowed himself to suffer on account of our life, how did he allow himself to suffer by a human hand? Learn now! ₆The prophets, receiving grace from him, prophesied concerning him. He had to be manifested in human flesh in order to destroy death and show forth the resurrection from the dead. ₇He allowed himself to suffer in order that he might redeem the promises to our ancestors and, while preparing a new people for himself, to show, on the earth, that he would himself carry out judgement after raising the dead. ₈Finally, when he was teaching Israel and performing such signs and wonders, they had no great love for him through his proclamation.[37] ₉When he chose his own apostles, who were lawless beyond all sin, who would proclaim the Gospel, so he showed that he had not come to call the righteous but sinners, then he manifested himself to be the Son of God. ₁₀Had he not come in the flesh, how then would people be saved in looking upon him, when they cannot fix their eyes or focus their gaze directly upon the sun, which will cease to be and which is the work of his hands?

₁₁For this reason, therefore, the Son of God came in the flesh,— that he might total up the sum of the sins of those who persecuted his prophets to the death,—₁₂for this reason he allowed it. For God says that the beating of his flesh should be at their hands. "When they have struck their shepherd, then shall the sheep of the flock perish." (Zech 13.7) ₁₃He himself desired to suffer in this manner, for he had

[37]The text is very corrupt and its meaning uncertain. There is a welter of variant readings and editorial conjectures.

to suffer upon a tree. For of him the prophet said: "Deliver my life from the sword" and "fix my flesh with nails because assemblies of evildoers have risen up against me." (Ps 21.21, 17) ₁₄And again he says: "Look, I have set my back to the whips and my cheeks to blows, and I have set my face like a hard rock." (Is 50.6–7)

6   ₁So, when he established the commandment, what did he say? "Who is in judgement over me? Stand up against me! Who considers himself just before me? Let him approach the servant of the Lord! ₂Woe to you because you will all grow old like a garment and a moth will consume you." (Is 50.8–9) And again, because he was like a strong stone set to crush, the prophet says: "Look, I shall set in the foundations of Zion a precious stone, chosen, a cornerstone, honourable." ₃Then what does he say? "The one who believes in him shall live for ever." (Is 28.16) Is our hope, then, set on a stone? Not at all, but rather because our Lord has set his flesh in strength. For he says: "He set me up as a hard rock." (Is 50.7) ₄Again the prophet says: "The stone which the builders rejected has become the head of the corner." And again he says: "This is the great and wonderful day which the Lord made." (Ps 117. 22, 24) ₅I am writing to you very simply so that you may understand. I am the devoted slave of your love. ₆What does the prophet say again: "An assembly of evildoers surrounded me, they encircled me like bees round a honeycomb" and "They cast lots upon my clothing." (Pss 21.17, 117.12, 21.19) ₇Thus he showed his passion in advance when he was going to appear himself in flesh and suffer. For the prophet says of Israel: "Woe to their lives, because they hatched a wicked plot against themselves, saying: 'Let us tie up the just one because he is troublesome to us.'" (Is 3.9–10)

₈What does Moses, the other prophet, say to them? "Look, the Lord says this. 'Go forth into the good land which the Lord promised to Abraham and Isaac and Jacob and divide it up, as it is flowing with milk and honey.'" (Ex 33.1,3) ₉What does insight say? Learn this. "Put your hope," it says, "in Jesus, who is going to appear to you in the flesh." For a human being is land which has feelings, as the formation of Adam was from the substance of the earth. ₁₀Why then does he say "Into the good land . . . flowing with milk and honey"? Blessed is our Lord, brothers, who has put into us wisdom and understanding of his secrets! For the prophet says: "Who will understand a parable of the Lord, except the one who is wise and knowledgeable and loving towards his Lord?"

₁₁He has thus renewed us in the remission of sins, making us in another pattern, as though our lives were that of an infant, making us completely anew. ₁₂For Scripture is speaking of us, as he says to the Son: "Let us make humanity after our image and likeness, and it should rule over the beasts of the earth and the birds of the sky and the fish of the sea." (Gen 1.26) And the Lord said, in looking upon our good creation: "Increase and multiply and fill the earth." (Gen 1.28) This was said to the Son.

₁₃Again I will show you how he speaks to us. He made a new creation in the most recent times. The Lord says: "Look, I am making the first like the last." For this reason the prophet proclaimed: "Enter into the land which is flowing with milk and honey and govern it." (Ex 33.3) ₁₄Therefore see, those who have been formed anew, how again in another prophet he says: " 'Look,' the Lord says, 'I shall take from them (that is, from those whom the Holy Spirit foresaw) the hearts of stone and put in those of flesh,' " (Ezek 11.19) because he himself would appear in the flesh and dwell among us. ₁₅For the holy temple to the Lord, my brothers, is his dwelling in our hearts. ₁₆For again the Lord says: "In what shall I appear to the Lord my God and be glorified?" (Ps 41.3) He says: "I shall confess to you in the assembly of my brothers, and I shall sing to you in the midst of the assembly of the saints." (Ps 21.23) Therefore, those he brought into the good earth are we ourselves.

₁₇What, therefore, is the "milk" and the "honey"? Because first an infant is sustained on honey, and then on milk, so we too, sustained by faith in the promise and by the word, shall live, governing the earth. ₁₈It was already said, above: "Let them increase and multiply and rule over the fish." (Gen 1.28) How, now, is he able to rule over the beasts or the fish or the birds of the sky? We should comprehend this, as to rule implies authority, so that the one who issues commands is the one who has governance. ₁₉Even if this is not occurring now he has told us when it will happen,—that is when we are ourselves perfected and allowed participation in the covenant of the Lord.

7   ₁So understand, children of gladness, that the good Lord has revealed all things to us in advance, so that we might know whom above all we should praise in giving thanks. ₂Thus if the Son of God, who is Lord and will come to judge the living and the dead, suffered in order that his beating might bring life to us, we should believe that the Son of God was not able to suffer except on our behalf. ₃But being crucified he drank of vinegar and gall. Hear how the priests of the temple revealed this, as the commandment was written: "Whoever does not fast in the fast (of atonement) shall be condemned to death." (Lev 23.29) The Lord commanded because he was himself to offer the vessel of the spirit as a sacrifice on account of our sins. Thus was the representation, which was shown forth in Isaac offered on the altar, brought to completion. ₄Now what does it say in the prophet? "Let them eat of the goat which is offered for all sins at the fast." Pay careful attention: " . . . and the priests alone should all eat the intestines unwashed, with vinegar." ₅Why so? "Since I am to offer my flesh on behalf of the sins of my new people, while you offer me gall to drink, mixed with vinegar, you alone are to eat, while the people is fasting and mourning in sack-cloth and ashes." So he demonstrates that he would suffer at their hands. ₆How does he command? Pay attention. "Take two fine goats which are similar and offer them, and let the priest take one as a whole-burnt offering for sins." (Lev 16.7,9) ₇What will they do with the other one? "The other," he says, "is cursed." (Lev 16.8) Observe carefully how the representation of Jesus is revealed. 8"And all will spit on it and pierce it and wrap a scarlet skein around its head, and so it should be cast into the wilderness." (Lev 16.10) And when this happens the one who takes the goat leads it into the wilderness and removes the skein and places it on a bush

called a blackberry, of the buds of which we are accustomed to eat when we find it in the countryside. Thus the fruits of the blackberry alone are sweet.[38]

₉What does this mean then, that the first is for the altar, the other is accursed, and the one which is accursed is crowned? Listen. Because then they shall see him, on that day, wearing the scarlet robe around his flesh, and they shall say: "Is this not he whom once we crucified, rejecting him, piercing him and spitting upon him? Truly it was he who said that he was the Son of God." ₁₀How is he like that goat? For this reason. The goats shall be alike, beautiful, equal, in order that when they see him then emerging they may be astonished at the likeness of the goat. Therefore observe the representation. If Jesus he was destined to suffer, ₁₁why then do they put the wool between the horns? It is a representation of Jesus set within the church, because should anyone wish to remove the scarlet wool they must suffer greatly because the thorns are frightful, and only through pain can anyone attain it. Thus, he says, "Those who want to see me and attain to my Kingdom should lay hold on me through pain and suffering."

8   ₁What then, do you suppose it represents when he commands Israel that men who are thoroughly sinful should offer a heifer, and burn it when it is slaughtered, and that then children should take the ashes and put them in containers and then wrap scarlet wool around a piece of wood (observe, again, the representation of the cross and the scarlet wool) and the hyssop, and that the children should thus sprinkle the people one by one so that they might be purified from their sins. Understand how he speaks to you in simplicity . . . ₂The calf is Jesus. The men who are sinners who make the offering are those who offered him for slaughter. Then they are men no longer, and the glory of sinners is no more. ₃The children who sprinkle are those to whom he gave authority to proclaim the Gospel, who announce to us the good news of the remission of sins and the puri-

---

[38]The precise fruit-bush which is meant is not clear, but the overall meaning is clear enough; it is a sweet fruit which grows on a thorny bush.

fication of the heart. They are twelve, bearing witness to the tribes, because there were twelve tribes of Israel. ₄Why then are the children who sprinkle three? As a witness to Abraham, Isaac, Jacob, because these were great in the sight of God. ₅Why then is the wool on the wood? Because the kingdom of Jesus is on the wood and those who hope in him shall live for ever. ₆Why the wool and the hyssop at the same time? Because in his Kingdom there shall be wicked days and foul, in which we shall be saved, because anyone who is sick in the body is healed by the foulness of the hyssop. ₇And thus what has happened to us is clear in this way to us, but obscure to them because they have not heard the voice of the Lord.

9 ₁For again he speaks regarding the ears, how he circumcised our hearts. The Lord says in the prophet: "They obeyed me through hearing with their ears" (Ps 17.45) And again he says: "'Those who are far away will hear clearly, what I have done they will know. And circumcise your ears,' says the Lord." (Is 33.13) ₂And again he says, "Listen Israel, the Lord your God says this to you. Who is it who wishes to live for ever? He should pay careful attention to the voice of my servant." (Is 50.10) ₃And again he says; "Listen heaven and earth, prick up your ears, because the Lord has spoken these things as bearing witness." (Is 1.2) And again he says: "Listen to the voice of the Lord, you rulers of this people." (Is 1.10) And again he says: "Hear, children, the voice of one crying out in the wilderness." (Is 40.3) Thus he has circumcised our ears so that we, hearing the word, may have faith.

₄But also the circumcision in which they put their trust has been rejected. For he states that circumcision should not be of the flesh, but that they transgressed because a wicked angel was leading them astray. ₅For He speaks to them: "This is what the Lord your God says to you," here I declare a commandment, "do not sow among thorns but be circumcised for your Lord." (Jer 4.3–4) And what does he mean? "And circumcise the wickedness from your hearts"?[39] Again

---

[39]The text of Kraft, who here prefers the Latin version, is followed, but note that

he says: "Look, the Lord is speaking: All the nations have uncircumcised foreskins, but this nation is uncircumcised in its heart." (Jer
9.26) ₆But you will say, "Surely the people is circumcised as a mark
of ownership?" But, indeed, so is every Syrian and Arab and all the
priests of the idols—are these also within their covenant? Even the
Egyptians are within circumcision.

₇Therefore learn, beloved children, richly concerning all this.
Abraham, the first to practise circumcision, circumcised as he
looked forward, in the spirit, to Jesus, receiving the teaching of three
letters. ₈For it says. "And Abraham circumcised eighteen and three
hundred men of his household." (Gen 14.14) What insight was given
to him? Learn. First "eighteen" and then, after a pause, "three hundred." The eighteen is I, ē,—you have Je(sus), yet because the cross,
shown in the T, would possess grace, he then says "three hundred."
So he makes Jesus manifest in the first two letters and the cross in the
other.[40] ₉The one who placed this gift of instruction[41] in us knows
this. Nobody has learnt anything better than this from me, but I
know that you are worthy.

10 ₁Because Moses said "You shall not eat pig, nor eagle, nor hawk,
nor crow nor any fish which does not have scales upon itself" (Lev
11.7–15; Deut 14.8–14) he received three teachings in his understanding. ₂Moreover he said to them in Deuteronomy: "And I shall set out
my demands for this people." (Deut 4.10, 13) Thus the commandment of God is not a matter of what not to eat, as Moses spoke in
the spirit. ₃Pig, he stated for this reason: " Do not associate," he says,
"with such people who are like pigs." That is to say, when they are
living luxuriously they are forgetful of the Lord, but when they are
in need they are mindful of the Lord. So, also, is the pig: when it is

the Greek versions all cite Deut 10.16 instead: "Circumcise your hardened hearts and
do not stiffen your necks."

[40]Greek represented numbers by letters. Eighteen is represented by i and ē, the
first two letters of the name of Jesus in Greek, and three-hundred by T, which looks
like a cross in Greek, as well as in Latin, script.

[41]Some MSS have "covenant".

eating it does not know its master but when it is hungry it cries out, and is silent again when it gets its food. ₄"You shall not eat," he says, "the eagle, the hawk, the kite or the crow." (Lev 11.13–16) You shall not, he is saying, associate with nor be similar to such people, who do not know how to gain food for themselves through labour and sweat, but grasp others' in their lawlessness, and are always on the watch as they go around with an air of innocence to see what they can plunder in their greed. These are the only birds which do not gain their food by themselves but sit by idly, seeking out how they might devour others' meat. They are pestilential in their wickedness. ₅"And you shall not eat," he says, "the lamprey, the octopus or the cuttlefish." Do not, he says, be like to or associates of such people, who are utterly impious and who are condemned to death already. For these fish alone are accursed, and hover in the depths, not swimming like the others, but dwelling in the mud beneath the depths. ₆"But also do not eat the hare." (Lev 11.6) Why not? He is saying that you should not be a corrupter of children nor be anything like such people, because the rabbit adds an orifice each year, having as many holes as it has years alive. ₇"Nor should you eat the hyena." You are not, he says, to become an adulterer or a corrupter or be like such people. Why so? Because this animal changes its nature on an annual basis, and is first male, then female. ₈But also he despises the weasel. Rightly. He is saying that one should not become such, nor be like those who, we hear, in their impurity commit lawlessness in the mouth, nor associate with those impure women who perform the lawless act with their mouths. For this animal conceives in its mouth. ₉Moses, receiving three teachings concerning foodstuffs spoke in the spirit, yet in the desire of their flesh they understood him to be speaking about food.

₁₀David received insight into the same three teachings and speaks thus: "Happy is the one who has not set forth in the counsel of the impious", (Ps 1.1) just as fish go forth into the depths in darkness. "Nor stood in the way of sinners." Just as those who appear to fear the Lord yet sin are as the pig. "Nor sat on the chair of the pestilent." Just as birds sit, ready to swoop. You have it put perfectly, concerning foodstuffs.

₁₁But Moses said: "Eat every animal which is cloven-hoofed and chews the cud." (Lev 11.3; Deut 14.6) Why does he say this? Because such an animal, in receiving nourishment, knows who is nourishing it and appears to rejoice in him as it rests. He spoke well, as we examine the commandment. What then does he mean? Associate with those who fear the Lord, with those who meditate in their hearts on the meaning of the word which they have received, with those who speak the righteous commands of the Lord and keep them, with those who see that meditation is a joyous deed and who ruminate on the word of the Lord. Why then "cloven-hoofed?" Because the one who is just goes around in this world whilst waiting for the age of holiness. See how Moses legislated so well. ₁₂But where will they gain knowledge or understanding of these things? We, however, are speaking of the commandments in the proper way, as the Lord desired. Therefore he circumcised our ears and our hearts so that we might have this understanding.

11   ₁We may examine whether the Lord intended to reveal anything in advance concerning the water and concerning the cross. It is written of Israel regarding the water that they would not accept the baptism which brings the remission of sins, but would construct something for themselves. ₂For the prophet says: "Be astonished, heaven, and earth shake yet more at this, for this people has done two wicked things. They have deserted me, the fountain of life,[42] and have dug for themselves a channel of death. ₃Is Sinai, my holy mountain, a deserted rock? For you will be as the young of a bird, taken from their nest and fluttering around." (Jer 2.12–13) ₄And again the prophet says: "I shall set out before you and I shall flatten mountains and I shall crush gates of bronze and I shall shatter bars of iron and I shall give you treasures which are dark, hidden, unseen, so that you may know that I am the Lord God" (Is 45.2–3) ₅and "You shall

---

[42]Some MSS have "living water".

dwell in a high cave of strong rock and its water will be unfailing. You will see a King with glory, and your life shall consider the fear of the Lord." (Is 33.16–18) ₆And again he speaks in another prophet: "Whoever does these things shall be like the tree which is planted beside the flowing waters. It will give its fruit at the proper time, and its leaf shall not fall and whatever it does shall be prospered. ₇Not so the impious, not so, but like the chaff, which the wind blows away from the face of the earth. Therefore the impious shall not rise up in judgement nor sinners in the counsel of the righteous, because the Lord knows the way of the just and the way of the impious shall be destroyed." (Ps 1.3–6) ₈Observe how the water and the cross occur at the same place. For he means that those who went down into the water putting their hope in the cross are fortunate, because, as he says, there shall be a reward at the proper time. Then, he says, shall I pay. Now, as he says "the leaves shall not fall", he means this: that every saying which emerges from you by your mouth in faithfulness and love shall lead to conversion and hope for many.

₉And again, another prophet says: "And the land of Jacob was praised beyond any other land." It means this: he glorifies the vessel of his spirit. ₁₀Then what does he say? "And there was a river flowing from its right, and beautiful trees were growing from it. And whoever ate of them would live eternally." (Ezek 47.1–12) ₁₁This means that we go down into the water covered in sins and filth and emerge bearing fruit of fear in our hearts and having hope in Jesus in our spirits. "And whoever ate of them would live for ever." This means that he is saying that whoever hears what is said and believes shall live eternally.

12 ₁Likewise he declares again concerning the cross in another prophet, who says: "'And when will these things be brought to completion?', says the Lord. 'When a tree falls and rises up and when blood flows from a tree.'" (4 Ezra 4.33; 5.5) Again you have it concerning the cross and the one who would be crucified. ₂He speaks again to Moses when Israel is being attacked by a foreign nation so as to remind those who were being attacked that they were being handed over to death on account of their sins. The Spirit speaks to Moses' heart that he should make a representation of the cross and of the one who would suffer so, he says, that should they not hope in him then they will be attacked to eternity. Therefore Moses, in the middle of the fight, stacked weapons one upon the other and, stationing himself higher than all others, stretched out his hands, and so Israel again became victorious. But then, when he lowered them, they began to be killed.[43] ₃Why this? So that they might know that they could not be saved unless they put their hope in him. ₄And again he speaks in another prophet: "I have stretched out my hands for the entire day towards a disbelieving people which opposes my righteous way." (Is 65.2) ₅Again Moses makes the representation of Jesus, of the suffering that he would have to undergo, and of his own bestowal of life, him whom they shall believe to have been destroyed. This was in a sign when Israel was falling. For the Lord caused every serpent to bite them and, since the transgression occurred in Eve by means of the serpent, they were dying. So he convinced them that they were being handed over to the affliction of death on account of their transgression. ₆Even though Moses himself commanded "there shall be nothing which is molten or carved as your God," (Lev 26.1; Deut 27.5) he himself made one in order to show forth the representation of Jesus. Thus Moses made a bronze serpent and put it in a prominent position and called the people with a proclamation. ₇Thus when they came at this proclamation they begged Moses to offer up a prayer for them so that they should be healed. Moses spoke to them stating: "Any of you, when bitten, should come to the serpent which is displayed on the tree and hope, believing, that although it is dead it can bring about life, and straightway be saved." And so they did. Once again you have the glory of Jesus in these things, because all things are in him and for him. ₈Again, why does Moses say to Jesus, the son of Nave, when he gave him this name, as he was a prophet, that the entire people should listen to him alone? Because

[43]Ex 17.8–13.

the Father reveals everything concerning Jesus his Son.[44] ₉So Moses says to Jesus, the son of Nave, when he gave him this name, when he sent him to reconnoitre the land, "Take a book in your hands and write down what the Lord says, that in the last days the Son of God will chop down the entire house of Amalek at its roots." (Ex 17.14) ₁₀Again, observe Jesus, not as son of man but as Son of God manifestly represented in flesh. Thus, since they are going to say that the messiah is the son of David, David himself prophesies in fear and in understanding of the error of sinners. "The Lord said to my Lord, sit at my right hand, until I make your enemies a footstool for your feet." (Ps 109.1) ₁₁And again Isaiah speaks thus: "The Lord said to Christ my Lord, 'I have grasped his right hand so that the nations shall be obedient before him. And I will shatter the power of kings.'" (Is 45.1) See how David refers to him as Lord, and does not refer to him as his son.

13 ₁Let us see now, whether it is this people which is the heir or the first, and whether the covenant is for us or for them.

₂Listen therefore to what Scripture says regarding the people: "Isaac interceded for Rebecca his wife because she was barren, and she conceived. Then Rebecca went out to consult the Lord, and the Lord said to her: 'Two nations are in your belly and two peoples in your womb, and one people shall obtain dominance over the other people and the greater shall serve the lesser.'" (Gen 25.21–23) ₃You must understand, who is Isaac and who is Rebecca and what he is intending when he says that "this" people is greater than "that."

₄And in another prophecy Jacob addresses himself more clearly to Joseph his son as he says: "Look, the Lord has not deprived me of your presence. Bring me your sons so that I may bless them." (Gen 48.11,9) ₅And He brought Ephraim and Manasseh, wishing that Manasseh should receive the blessing, as he was the older. Joseph led them to the right hand of his father Jacob. In the spirit, Jacob saw a representation of the people which was to be. And what does it say:

---

[44]Jesus is the Greek form of Joshua.

"And Jacob crossed his hands and put his right hand on the head of Ephraim, the second and younger and blessed him. And Joseph said to Jacob: 'Put your right hand on the head of Manasseh, because he is my firstborn son.' And Jacob said to Joseph: 'I know, son, I know. But the greater shall serve the lesser, and this is the one who will be blessed.'" (Gen 48.14,19) ₆You see he has laid it down that this people should be first and the heir of the covenant

₇Our insight is reaching perfection if we recall that this was so in the case of Abraham. Thus what did he say to Abraham when he alone in believing was established in righteousness? "Look, I have established you, Abraham, as the father of nations who, in uncircumcision, put their trust in God." (Gen 15.6; 17.4)

14   ₁Indeed so. But we should see whether he has actually given the covenant which he swore to the ancestors that he would give to the people. We must explore this. He gave it, but they were not worthy to receive it on account of their sins. ₂For the prophet says: "Moses was fasting on the Mountain of Sinai for forty days and forty nights so that he could receive the covenant of the Lord for the people." (Ex 24.18) And Moses received the two tablets which were inscribed by the finger of the hand of the Lord in the spirit. Moses received them and carried them down to give to the people. ₃And the Lord spoke to Moses: "Moses, Moses, get down quickly, because your people, whom you brought out of the land of Egypt, has been lawless." And Moses understood that once again they had made for themselves molten images and he threw the tablets from his hands, and the tablets of the covenant of the Lord were broken. ₄So Moses received it, but they were not worthy. How then do we receive it? Learn now. Moses was a servant when he received it, but the Lord himself gave it to us, as heirs to the people, through his endurance on our behalf. ₅He was made manifest in order that they might be made complete in their sins, and that we might inherit by means of the one who inherited the covenant, Jesus Christ. He was made ready so that, in becoming manifest, he might establish a covenant within us by his word, having ransomed our hearts, which were already paid over to death and betrayed to the lawlessness of deceit, from darkness. ₆For it is written how the Father commanded him to prepare for himself a holy people from us who were ransomed from darkness. ₇Therefore the prophet says: "I, the Lord your God, called you in righteousness and I shall grasp your hand and I shall strengthen you. And I have given you as a covenant of the people, as a light for the nations, to open the eyes of the blind and lead from bondage those were in chains and those seated in darkness from a prison." (Is 42.6–7) So it is that we know from whence we have been ransomed.

₈Again the prophet says: "Look, I have set you up as a light to the nations so that you may be salvation as far as the end of the earth. So says the Lord, the God who ransoms you." (Is 49.6–7) ₉And again the prophet says: "The Spirit of the Lord is upon me and he has anointed me for this reason: to announce grace to the humble. He has sent me to heal those who are crushed in their hearts, to proclaim release for captives and renewed sight to the blind, to call out the year which is acceptable to the Lord and the day of recompense, to strengthen all those who are mourning." (Is 61.1–2)

15 ₁In the ten words, in which he spoke to Moses face to face on Mount Sinai, yet more is written concerning the Sabbath. "And you shall sanctify the Sabbath of the Lord with pure hands and a pure heart." (Ex 20.8) ₂Elsewhere he says: "If my children keep the Sabbath then I shall bestow my mercy upon them." (Jer 17.24–25) ₃The Sabbath of which he is speaking is at the foundation of creation. "God performed the works of his hands in six days, and completed them on the seventh day and rested on it and sanctified it." (Gen 2.2–3) ₄Pay attention, children, to what it means by completion in six days. It means that the Lord will complete all things in six thousand years, for with him a day indicates a thousand years. He himself supports me when he says: "Look, a day of the Lord will be like a thousand years." (Ps 89.4) And so, children, everything shall be made complete in six days, that is in six thousand years. ₅And he

rested on the seventh day. That means that when his Son comes he
shall put an end to the age of the lawless one and shall judge the impious and shall alter the sun and the moon and the stars. Then shall he
rest indeed on the seventh day. ₆Moreover, it says "You shall sanctify
it with pure hands and a pure heart." Now if anyone can sanctify the
day which God has sanctified by being pure in heart at this present
time we are grossly in error. ₇Observe that it is[45] when we are properly at rest that we shall sanctify it, and we will be able to do so then
as we ourselves will be made righteous and we shall have received
the promise, as lawlessness is no more, and as all things are renewed
by the Lord. It is then that we shall be able to sanctify it, as we shall
ourselves have been sanctified first. ₈Moreover he says to them: "I
despise your new moons and your Sabbaths." (Is 1.13) You see what
he means: It is not the present Sabbaths which are acceptable to me
but that which I have made, in which I shall give rest to everything
and make a beginning on the eighth day, which is the beginning of
another world. ₉Thus we also observe the eighth day in gladness,
the day on which Jesus was raised from the dead and appeared and
ascended into the heavens.

16   ₁I still wish to speak to you about the temple, about the manner in which those unfortunates, in their error, placed their hope in
a building, as though it were the house of God, and not in their God
who made them. ₂They were almost like the gentiles in hallowing
him within the temple. But how does the Lord speak in denying it?
Learn now! " 'Who has measured the heaven with a hand, or the
earth with his fingers? Is it not I,' says the Lord. 'The heaven is my
throne, the earth is a footstool for my feet. What kind of house could
you build for me, or in what place should I take my rest?' " (Is 40.12;
66.1) You have recognized, then, that their hope is vain. ₃Moreover
he says again: "Look, those who destroyed this temple will build it
themselves." (Is 49.17) ₄This is occurring. For due to the war they
conducted it was destroyed by their enemies. And now they, who

[45]Cf. Kraft and Prigent's reading and conjecture: "If we do not do so now . . ."

are servants to their enemies, will build it themselves. ₅Again it was revealed how the city and the temple and the people of Israel would be abandoned. For Scripture says: "It shall come about in the last days that the Lord will abandon the sheep of the pasture and the enclosure and watchtower." (1 Enoch 89.56) And it has occurred in accordance with what the Lord said.

₆Let us then enquire whether there is indeed a temple of God. There is one, where he says that he is making it and completing it. For it is written: "It will come about, at the completion of the seventh day, that a temple of God will be gloriously built in the name of the Lord." (Dan 9.24; 1 Enoch 91.13) ₇I so discover that there is a temple. How then is it to be built upon the name of the Lord? Learn now. Before we believed in God the dwelling place of our heart was corrupt and weak, as it really was a temple built by hand, because it was full of idolatry and was a house of demons because we did everything that was opposed to God. ₈But it will be built upon the name of the Lord. So pay attention so that the temple of the Lord may be gloriously built. How? Learn. As we receive the remission of sins and put our hope in the name of the Lord we are made new, created again from the beginning. Thus God truly dwells in the dwelling place which is within us. ₉How? His word of fidelity, his call to us in the promise, the wisdom of his decrees, the commandments of the teaching, himself prophesying in us, himself dwelling in us who were enslaved to death, opening the door of the temple which is ours, that is the mouth. Granting us repentance, he leads us towards an incorruptible temple. ₁₀Somebody who longs to be saved does not look simply to a human being but to the one who is dwelling in him and speaking, and does so in amazement since the words which he is speaking have never before been heard from his mouth. He did not even desire to hear them himself. This is a spiritual temple which is built of the Lord.

17   ₁My hope is that, in my enthusiasm, I have not omitted anything which is necessary to salvation, as I have, to the best of my ability, made you this simple demonstration. ₂For if I should write to you about things present or things to come you would not understand as they are set forth in parables. So this is sufficient.

18   ₁So let us turn to another form of insight and instruction. There are two ways of instruction and authority, that of light and that of darkness. The difference between the two ways is great. For over one are set light-bringing angels of God, over the other the angels of Satan. ₂And one is Lord from the ages and to the ages, the other is ruler over the present age of lawlessness.

19   ₁The way of light is this. Anyone who desires to travel the way to the place which is appointed should be diligent in his deeds. Such is the insight which has been given to us, that we may walk in it. ₂You shall love the one who made you, you shall fear the one who formed you, you shall glorify the one who ransomed you from death. Be simple in heart and rich in spirit. Do not associate with those who are going along on the way of death, you shall despise all that is not pleasing to God, you shall despise all hypocrisy. You should not forsake the commandments of the Lord. ₃You shall not make yourself haughty, you shall be humble-minded in every way. You shall not accrue glory for yourself. You should not plot evil against your neighbour, you shall not give your life over to presumption. ₄You shall not fornicate, you shall not commit adultery, you shall not despoil a child. The word of God is not to go out from you to any of the impure. You shall not show partiality in rebuking anyone for a transgression. You shall be generous, you shall be peaceable, fearing the words which you heard. Do not store up wrongs against your brother. ₅You shall not be divided in your mind, whether it will be or not. You should not take the name of the Lord for a futile purpose. You shall love your neighbour more than your own life. You shall not murder a child through abortion, nor, again, do away with it once born. You should not withdraw your hand from your son or from your daughter, but from their youth you shall teach the fear of God.

₆You should not be covetous of what belongs to your neighbour, you should not be grasping, nor should you spend your life with the exalted but associate with the righteous and lowly. Whatever befall you, accept these experiences as good, knowing that nothing occurs without God. ₇You shall not be double-minded nor double-tongued. For being double-tongued is a snare of death.

You should be subject to your masters in reverence and fear as a representation of God. You should not command your servant or your maid in a bitter manner, for they put their hope in the same God. Otherwise they may cease to fear the God who is set over both of you. Because he did not make his call with regard to persons but with respect to those whom the Spirit made ready. ₈You will share with your neighbour in all things and you shall not claim anything as your own. For if you are companions in what is incorruptible, are you not much more so with regard to what is perishable? You shall not be garrulous, for the mouth is a snare of death. As much as you are able be pure within. ₉Do not be one who stretches out hands to take, whilst retracting them to avoid giving. You shall love everyone who speaks the word of the Lord to you as the apple of your eye. ₁₀You should remember the day of judgement night and day, and you shall seek out each day the presence of the saints, either labouring through the word and going out to exhort and to be concerned to save a soul through the word or labouring with your hands as a ransom for your sins. ₁₁You shall not hesitate about giving, nor shall you grumble when giving; you know who is the good paymaster of the reward.

You shall preserve what you have received, neither adding nor subtracting. You shall absolutely despise evil. You shall judge justly.

₁₂You shall not bring about a schism, you shall reconcile those who are disputing by bringing them together. You should confess your transgression, you shall not come to prayer with an evil conscience. This is the way of the light.[46]

[46]This phrase is not present in all MSS and Kraft suggests that it is added in order to harmonize with the Didache.

20 ₁The way of the dark one is crooked and beset by cursing. For it is the way of everlasting death, alongside punishment, in which are the things which destroy lives. Idolatry, insolence, the glorification of power, hypocrisy, duplicity, adultery, murder, robbery, arrogance, transgression, trickery, malice, insolence, charms, sorcery, greed, disregard of God, ₂persecutors of the good, haters of the truth, lovers of falsehood, unaware of the reward for righteousness, not associating with the good, not with just judgement, with no regard for the widow or orphan, who lie awake not out of fear of God but for evil, from whom generosity and patience are distantly remote, loving foolishness, pursuing a reward, showing no pity to the poor, doing no labour for the downtrodden, prone to slander, unaware of the one who made them, murderers of children, corruptors of what God has formed, turning away the needy, treading down the afflicted, advocates of the rich, lawless judges of the poor, utterly sinful.

21 ₁And so it is good that one who has learnt the commands of the Lord, in as much as they are written, should walk in them. For the one who performs them shall be glorified in the Kingdom of God. The one who chooses otherwise will perish, along with his deeds. For this reason there is a resurrection, for this reason a reckoning. ₂I ask you who are foremost, if you are willing to receive any advice from my good counsel, keep with yourselves for whose good you may labour. Do not be wanting. ₃The day is near on which all things will perish alongside the evil one. The Lord is near, as is his reward. ₄I ask you again and again: Be good legislators for yourselves, remain faithful counsellors for yourselves, remove all hypocrisy from among you. ₅May God, who has dominion over the entire world, grant you wisdom, understanding, perception, knowledge of his commands, patience. ₆Be taught of God, seeking out what the Lord desires of you and so perform it that you may be found on the day of judgement. ₇If there is any recollection of what is good, remember me by practising these things, so that both desire and watchfulness may be put to good. I ask you this, asking a favour. ₈As long as the good vessel is with you do not fail in anything, but carefully seek them out and fulfil each demand. For they are worthy. ₉Thus I have been all the more anxious to write as I was able, to give you cause for rejoicing. Be well, children of love and peace. The Lord of Glory and of every grace be with your spirit.

A synoptic table of TWT in *D*, *L* and *B*

Didache	The teaching of the apostles	The letter of Barnabas
There are two ways, the one of life and the one of death;	There are two ways in the world, of life and death, of light and darkness. Two angels are set over them, the one of justice, the other of wickedness.	There are two ways of instruction and authority, that of light and that of darkness.
the difference between the ways is great.	For the difference between the two ways is great.	The difference between the two ways is great. For over one are set light-bringing angels of God, over the other the angels of Satan. And one is Lord from the ages and to the ages, the other is ruler over the present age of lawlessness.
Now the way of life is this.	Now the way of life is this.	The way of light is this. Anyone who desires to travel the way to the place which is appointed should be diligent in his deeds. Such is the insight which has been given to us, that we may walk in it. You shall love the one who made you, you shall fear the one who formed you, you shall glorify the one who ransomed you from
love the made you, First you shall God who	First you shall love the eternal God who made you,	

Didache	The teaching of the apostles	The letter of Barnabas
		death. (19.1–2b)
secondly your neighbour as yourself, and whatever you would not wish done to you, do not do to anyone else.	secondly your neighbour as yourself. Whatever you would not wish done to you, do not do to anyone else.	You shall love your neighbour more than your own life. (19.5c)
The instruction of these maxims is this: Bless those who curse you, and pray for your enemies, fast on behalf of those who persecute you. For what is the merit of loving those who love you? Do not even the gentiles do the same? But love those who hate you, and you shall have no enemy. Abstain from fleshly and worldly lusts. If any one gives you a blow to your right cheek, turn the other to him also, and you will be perfect. If anyone obliges you to go a mile, go with him two; if anyone takes away your cloak, give him your coat also. If anyone takes what is yours from you, do not ask for it back, for you are unable. Give to everyone who asks from you, and do not ask it back; for the Father wishes to give to all from his own graces. Whoever gives in accordance with the commandment is blessed, for he is free of guilt; but woe to anyone who receives. For anyone in need who receives is free of guilt; but	The meaning of these maxims is this:	

Didache	The teaching of the apostles	The letter of Barnabas
anyone who receives when not in need shall stand trial as to why he received and for what purpose; and when in prison shall be examined concerning the things that he has done, and shall not depart thence until he has paid back the last cent. But on this it was also said: "Let your alms sweat in your hands until you know to whom you are giving." The second commandment of the instruction: You shall not murder, you shall not commit adultery,	You shall not commit adultery, you shall not murder, you shall not bear false witness, you shall not despoil a child, you shall not fornicate,	You shall not fornicate, you shall not commit adultery,
you shall not despoil a child, you shall not fornicate, you shall not steal, you shall not practise sorcery, you shall not make potions, you shall not murder a child through abortion nor kill it	you shall not practise sorcery, you shall not make potions, you shall not destroy a child through abortion nor kill it	you shall not despoil a child. The word of God is not to go out from you to any of the impure. (19.4a-b) You shall not murder a child through abortion, nor, again, do away with it
once born, you shall not covet what is your neighbour's, you shall not swear falsely, you shall not bear false witness, you shall not speak evil, you shall not store up wrongs,	once born, you shall not covet what is your neighbour's. You shall not swear falsely. You shall not speak evil, you shall not store up wrongs,	once born. (19.5d) You should not be covetous of what belongs to your neighbour (19.6a) Do not store up wrongs against your brother. (19.4d)
you shall not be double-minded or double-tongued. For being double-tongued is a snare of death. Your word shall not be false, not empty, but shall be matched by action.	you shall not be double-minded in giving, nor double-tongued. For the tongue is a snare of death. Your word shall not be empty, nor false.	You shall not be double-minded nor double-tongued. For being double-tongued is a snare of death. (19.7a; cf. 19.8b)

Didache	The teaching of the apostles	The letter of Barnabas
You shall not be grasping, nor rapacious, nor hypocritical, nor malicious, nor arrogant. You shall not plot evil against your neighbour. You shall not hate any person, but some you shall rebuke, for some you shall pray, and some you shall love more than your own life.	You shall not be greedy nor grasping, nor rapacious, nor hypocritical, nor arrogant nor malicious. You shall not plot evil against your neighbour. You shall not hate any person, some you shall love more than your own life.	You should not be grasping (19.6a) You should not plot evil against your neighbour, (19.3b) (Cf. 19.5c above)
My child, shun every evil person and all who are like them. Do not be quick-tempered, for anger leads to murder, nor jealous nor quarrelsome nor aggressive. For murder is begotten from these. My child, do not be given over to passion, for lust leads to fornication, nor a speaker of base words, nor immodestly curious. For from all these adulteries are begotten. My child, do not be an examiner of omens, since this leads to idolatry, nor an enchanter nor an astrologer nor a lustrator,	Child, shun the evil person, and a person who is like to him. Do not be quick-tempered, for anger leads to murder, nor quarrelsome or aggressive. For anger is begotten from all of these. Do not be an astrologer, nor a lustrator, these things lead to empty superstition. Nor desire to see or hear.	
nor desire to see these things. For from all of these is idolatry begotten. My child, do not be a liar, since falsehood leads to theft, nor a lover of money nor vainglorious. For from all of these are thefts begotten. My child, do not be a grumbler, since it leads to blasphemy. Be not	Do not be a liar, since falsehood leads to theft, nor a lover of money nor vain glory. From all of these are thefts begotten. Do not be a grumbler, since it leads to blasphemy. Be not	

Didache	The teaching of the apostles	The letter of Barnabas
self-willed or evil-minded, for from all of these are blasphemies begotten. Be generous, since the generous shall inherit the earth. Be patient, merciful, guileless and peaceable, good and fearing always the words which you heard. You shall not make yourself haughty,	self-willed or evil-minded, for from all of these are blasphemies begotten. Be generous, since the generous will possess the sacred earth. Be patient in difficulty, good and fearing all the words which you hear. You shall not make yourself haughty, nor make yourself honourable among people,	You shall be generous, you shall be peaceable, fearing the words which you heard. (19.4d) You shall not make yourself haughty, you shall be humble-minded in every way. You shall not accrue glory for yourself. You should not plot evil against your neighbour. You shall
nor give your life over to presumption. Do not spend your life with the exalted but associate with the righteous and lowly. Whatever befall you, accept these experiences as good, knowing that nothing occurs without God. My child, you shall remember both night and day the one who speaks the word of God to you. You shall honour him as a master. For inasmuch as the dominion is discussed, the Lord is there. You shall seek out daily the presence of the saints, that you may find refreshment in their words.	nor give your life over to presumption. Do not spend your life with the exalted but associate with the righteous and lowly. Whatever mishaps befall you, accept these experiences as good, knowing that nothing occurs without God. You shall remember day and night the one who speaks the word of the Lord God to you. You shall honour him as a master. Whence what is of the Lord proceeds, the Lord is there. Seek out the presence of the saints, that you may find refreshment in their words.	not give your life over to presumption. (19.3) ... nor should spend your life with the exalted but associate with the righteous and lowly. Whatever befall you, accept these experiences as good, knowing that nothing occurs without God. (19.6.a-b) You shall love everyone who speaks the word of the Lord to you as the apple of your eye. You should remember the day of judgement night and day, and you shall seek out each day the presence of the saints, either labouring through the word and going out to exhort and to be concerned to save a soul through the word or labouring with your

Didache	The teaching of the apostles	The letter of Barnabas
		hands as a ransom for your sins. (19.9b-10)
You shall not bring about schism, you shall reconcile those who are disputing,	You shall not bring about schism, reconcile those who are disputing,	You shall not bring about schism, you shall reconcile those who are disputing by bringing them together. (19.12a) You shall judge justly. (19.11d)
you shall judge justly, you shall not show partiality in rebuking any transgression.	judge justly, knowing that you will be judged. You shall not defraud anyone in his business.	You shall not show partiality in rebuking anyone for a transgression. (19.4c)
You shall not be divided in your mind, whether it will be or not.	You shall not be doubtful whether it will be or not.	You shall not be divided in your mind, whether it will be or not. (19.5a)
Do not be one who stretches out hands to take, whilst retracting them to avoid giving. If you have possessions by means of your hands, you shall give a ransom for your sins.	Do not be one who stretches out a hand to take, whilst retracting to avoid giving back. If you have gained by means of your hands a ransom for your sins,	Do not be one who stretches out hands to take, whilst retracting them to avoid giving. (19.9a) Cf. 19.10 supra.
You shall not hesitate about giving, nor shall you grumble when giving, for you know who is the good paymaster of rewards.	you shall not hesitate about giving nor shall you grumble when giving, for you know who is the good paymaster of this reward.	You shall not hesitate about giving, nor shall you grumble when giving; you know who is the good paymaster of the reward. (19.11)
You shall not turn away a beggar. You shall share in common all things with your brother, and you shall not claim anything as your own. For if you are companions in immortality, are you not much more so in mortal matters?	You shall not turn your back upon a beggar. You shall share in common all things with your brothers, and you shall not claim anything as your own. For if we are companions in immortality, how much more should we go on from there. For the Lord desires that we should give to all out of his gifts.	You shall share all things with your neighbour and you shall not claim anything as your own. For if you are companions in what is incorruptible, are you not much more so with regard to what is perishable? (19.8a)
You shall not withdraw your hand from your son or from your daughter, but from their youth you shall	You shall not withdraw your hand from your children, but from their youth you shall	You should not withdraw your hand from your son or from your daughter, but from their youth you shall

Didache	The teaching of the apostles	The letter of Barnabas
teach them the fear of God.	teach them the fear of the Lord.	teach the fear of God.
You shall not command your servant or your maid, who put their hope in the same God, in bitterness, otherwise they may cease to fear the God who is set over both of you.	You shall not command your servant or your maid in rage; they put their hope in the same God. He should fear both God and you.	You should not command your servant or your maid in a bitter manner, for they put their hope in the same God. Otherwise they may cease to fear the God who is set over both of you.
For he does not make his call with regard to status, but with respect to those whom the Spirit made ready. You who are slaves shall be subject to your masters in reverence and fear as a representation of God.	For he does not make his call with regard to status, but those in whom he finds the Spirit. You who are slaves are to be subject to your masters in reverence and fear as a representation of God.	Because he did not make his call with regard to persons but with respect to those whom the Spirit made ready. (19.7c) You should be subject to your masters in reverence and fear as a representation of God. (19.7b) Be simple in heart and rich in spirit. Do not associate with those who are going along on the way of death,
You shall despise all hypocrisy, and everything that is not pleasing to the Lord. You shall not forsake the commandments of the Lord.	You shall despise all hypocrisy and you shall not do what is not pleasing to God.	you shall despise all that is not pleasing to God, you shall despise all hypocrisy. You should not forsake the commandments of the Lord. (19.2b-f)
You shall preserve what you have received, neither adding nor subtracting.	Child, preserve what you have heard, neither adding what is contrary to them, nor subtracting.	You shall preserve what you have received, neither adding nor subtracting. You shall absolutely despise evil. (19.11b-c)
You shall confess your transgressions in the assembly, and you shall not come to prayer with an evil conscience. This is the way	You shall not come to prayer with an evil conscience. This is the way	You should confess your transgression, you shall not come to prayer with an evil conscience. This is the way

Didache	The teaching of the apostles	The letter of Barnabas
of life.	of life.	of the light. (19.12b-c)
Yet the way of death is this.	For the way of death is opposed to it.	The way of the dark one is crooked and
First of all it is evil and beset by cursing.	Firstly it is evil and beset by cursing,	beset by cursing. For it is the way of everlasting death, alongside punishment, in which are the things which destroy lives. Idolatry, insolence, the glorification of power, hypocrisy, duplicity,
Murders, adulteries, lusts, fornications, thefts, idolatries, charms, sorceries, magic, robberies, falsities of witness, hypocrisies, double-heartedness, trickery, arrogance, malice,	adulteries, murders, falsities of witness, fornications, wrongful lusts, sorceries, wicked potions, thefts, vain superstitions, grasping, hypocrisies, contempt,	adultery, murder, robbery, arrogance, transgression, trickery, malice, insolence, charms, sorcery,
	malice,	
selfishness, greed, base speech, jealousy, insolence, haughtiness and pretence, persecutors of the good, haters of the truth, lovers of falsity, unaware of the reward for righteousness, not associating with the good or with just judgement.	insolence, greed, base speech, jealousy, insolence, haughtiness and pretence, not fearing, persecutors of the good, haters of the truth, lovers of falsity, those unaware of the reward of veracity, not associating with the good or with just judgement.	greed, disregard of God, persecutors of the good, haters of the truth, lovers of falsehood, unaware of the reward for righteousness, not associating with the good, not with just judgement, with no regard for the widow or orphan, who lie
Those who lie awake, not for good but for evil, far from generosity or patience, loving foolishness,	Those who lie awake, not for good but for evil, far from generosity and close to pride,	awake not out of fear of God but for evil, from whom generosity and patience are distantly remote, loving foolishness,
pursuing a reward, showing no pity to the poor, doing no labour for the downtrodden,	pursuing a reward, showing no pity to the poor, not mourning for those who mourn,	pursuing a reward, showing no pity to the poor, doing no labour for the downtrodden, prone to

Didache	The teaching of the apostles	The letter of Barnabas
unaware of the one who made them, murderers of children, corrupters of what God has formed, turning away the needy, treading down the afflicted, advocates of the rich, lawless judges of the poor, utterly sinful. Children, may you be rescued from all of these.	unaware of the one who made them, murderers of their children, abortionists, turning away from good works, depriving the labourer, advocates of those who rob the just. Child, keep yourself from all of these.	slander, unaware of the one who made them, murderers of children, corruptors of what God has formed, turning away the needy, treading down the afflicted, advocates of the rich, lawless judges of the poor, utterly sinful.

CHAPTER THREE

The two ways in the third century

Introduction

We have seen that the fundamental use to which the TWT was put in early Christianity was that of the direction of catechumens. We have also seen that the origin of the tradition was fundamentally related to the conception of covenantal promise and direction, an original context on which the Christian communities built, as the tradition provided the basis for the covenantal stipulations which those being baptized, and particularly gentiles being baptized, accepted on entering the community of the new covenant. In later documents, however, such as those studied in this chapter, we find that that the tradition has become detached from its roots, and that the way of life has become a free-standing block of material which might be put to different uses.

In this chapter we present two third-century documents which demonstrate this. Each clearly employs a document of the δ tradition. We may be clear that *D* itself is not employed as the Gospel section is absent from both. We may also be clear that there is a relationship between these two documents as both put the material of the way of life into the mouths of the same apostles. These two documents are the *Apostolic Church Order*, sometimes called the *Ecclesiastical Canons of the Apostles*, abbreviated hereafter to *K*, and the *Epitome of the Apostolic Commands* (*E*).

I have recently argued at length that the nature of the relationship between the two is that both are versions of the same original, which depicted the gathering of the apostles and which attributed to them the material of the way of life.[1] This original I have termed κ. The two texts are presented in a synopsis at the end of this chapter; a short discussion may therefore suffice to demonstrate the point that they are derived from a common original, as the argument can be followed at length elsewhere. *E* and *K* are both derivatives of this same document, and *E* is not simply an abbreviation of *K*, any more than *K* is an expansion of *E*.

When one is faced by three clearly related documents one can map out the possible relationships on the basis of finding the middle term between them. Thus, for instance, if we were to see these three phrases in parallel documents:

A: The cat sat on the green mat.
B: The cat sat on the round green mat.
C: The cat sat on the round mat.

We can deduce that B is the middle term as it is the only sentence which has all the words in the other two. Neither A nor C can be the middle term because each misses out a word which is not in the other versions. When the middle term is known then the number of possible relationships between the three versions is limited.

1: A and C independently copied B (each leaving out a different word.)

2: A and C are independent versions, and B combined them.

3: A was first, and was copied (and supplemented) by B and B was then copied by C.

4: C was first and was copied (and supplemented) by B and B was then copied by A.

[1]In my *Apostolic Church Order*.

In this case the issue is that of determining what is the middle term within the δ tradition, as represented by *D*, *E* and *K*. In addition we know, in this instance, that *D* precedes *E* and *K*, and therefore certain logical possibilities may be excluded.

Thus we may note, as an example which allows us to establish the middle term, the commands put into the mouth of Nathanael:

E	K	D
Nathanael said: Do not be a liar,	Nathanael said: My child, do not be a liar, since falsehood leads to theft,	My child, do not be a liar, since falsehood leads to theft,
nor a lover of money nor vainglorious. From all of these thefts come about.	nor a lover of money nor vainglorious. For from all of these thefts begotten. My child,	nor a lover of money nor vainglorious. For from all of these thefts begotten. My child,
Do not be a grumbler, not impassioned,	do not be a grumbler, since it leads to	do not be a grumbler, since it leads to
not self-willed nor evil-minded, for from all of these blasphemies come about.	blasphemy, nor self-willed nor evil-minded. For from all of these are blasphemies begotten.	blasphemy; be not self-willed or evil-minded, for from all of these are blasphemies begotten.
Be generous, since the generous shall inherit the Kingdom of God;	Be generous, for the generous will inherit the Kingdom of the Heavens.	Be generous, since the generous shall inherit the earth.
be patient, merciful, a peacemaker, pure of heart, guileless, peaceable, good, preserving and fearing the words of God.	Be patient, merciful, a peacemaker, pure in heart from every evil, guileless and peaceable, good and guarding and fearing the words which you heard.	Be patient, merciful, guileless and peaceable, good and fearing always the words which you heard.

There are a number of differences between these three versions of what is clearly the same material. However the critical distinction lies in the term "pure in heart". This does not appear in *D* but appears in both *K* and *E*. This means that *D* is not the original on which the two drew, even though the original is part of the δ tradition.

If we then look at *E* and *K*, we may note that *E* does not introduce the saying "Do not be a liar" with "my child", whereas *D* and *K* both do, and that *E* reads "words of God" when *D* and *K* both read "words which you heard." This means that *K* cannot be derived from *E*. *K* is therefore the middle term.

Because we know that *D* is first, there are only three possible relationships:

1: δ was copied by *K* and *K* was then copied by *E*.
2: δ was independently copied by *K* and *E*.
3: *K* combined δ and *E*.

However, when we turn to the conclusions of *E* and *D* we can see that the first relationship is impossible. For whereas *D* and *E* are very close *K* has a different conclusion altogether. *E* and *D* alike have a *Haustafel* (a description of household duties), here setting out duties towards slaves and children, whereas *K*'s conclusion is eschatological and lacks the *Haustafel* altogether. *E's* conclusion was not, therefore, derived from *K* but from the δ tradition.

Thus either δ was independently copied by *K* and *E* or *K* combined δ and *E* (substituting its own conclusion.)

This second possibility is, however, a logical possibility only and is very unlikely in reality as this is not the manner in which ancient editors worked. Moreover we should note that *E* makes no sense as a document on its own. It is without context and without preamble and is, as such, unlikely to have come about on its own except as a rewriting of an existing work.

We are thus led to conclude that the relationship between *K* and *E* is that they are independent versions of a branch of the δ tradition.

It is not, however, the same δ that *D* accessed. There are a number of arguments which lead me to posit a further version of δ, but most critical is the fact that in *E* and *K* the material is attributed to various apostles. The common source must already have made that attribution. This is the document I termed κ.

We may therefore suggest that *E* is an abridgement of κ undertaken as an aid to those employing the material in teaching, in the same way that epitomes were made of major classical works for use in schools. Indeed, there is another version of this way of life to be found in a single manuscript[2] which may likewise be seen as an exercise in epitomization.

We may present this conclusion diagrammatically thus:

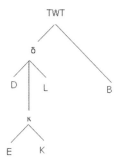

Not being in possession of κ it is uncertain whether, for instance, the way of death was also included (though its absence in *E* would probably indicate that it was not) or the context and rationale behind the apostolic attribution of the segments of the way of life. It is possible that direct apostolic witness was desired to support the tradition which, generally, was considered apostolic, as the third century was a period in which there was an almost romantic harking back to the apostolic period, as well as a time at which anchorage of teachings was sought through the identification of teachings with individual apostolic figures, particularly as the result of the literary struggle with gnosticism, which likewise claimed apostolic sanction for its teachings.

Such is certainly the rationale behind the adoption of κ by *K* since, apart from promulgating the way of life it is concerned to chart the manner in which the church should be organized, and is

[2]Namely *Codex Mosquensis* 125, this may be found edited at O. Gebhardt et al. (eds.) *Patrum apostolicorum opera* 1.2 (Leipzig: Hinrichs, 1878), XXIX–XXXI.

particularly concerned to regulate the ministry of women, largely by reducing the role of widows to a pastoral role, in a manner much reminiscent of the later deaconesses of the Syrian *Didascalia*.

The regulation of ministry is possibly also the reason why the content of κ, possibly with some expansions, prefaces the church order material. It is interesting that in the fourth century the material which was originally directed at catechumens comes to be directed towards clergy; thus canon 46 of the Council of Laodicea directs that "they who are of the priesthood, or of the clergy, shall not be magicians, enchanters, mathematicians, or astrologers; nor shall they make what are called amulets, which are chains for their own souls. And those who wear such, we command to be cast out of the Church." It is thus possible that K had read the material in the same light as the council, for which reason, despite the promise of hearing two ways in K4.1, only one way, that of life, is described. Similarly, Faivre notes the extent to which the qualifications laid down for the deacon in the latter part of K mirror the moral qualities besought in the Two Ways section,[3] and we may note that the same transference of qualities from catechumens to clergy has occurred in the *Didascalia*; "Let him not be double-minded or double-tongued", states the didascalist of the qualifications of the bishop, and in discussing the meekness of a young bishop seems to echo D3.7–8,[4]

There is a complication, however, in the neat picture of TWT in K being ultimately derived from δ, in that at several points in K the parallels are closer to B than to D or E. This has led some scholars to suggest that K has used B. However, I have argued in response that K was aware of a similar tradition to B, but did not use B itself. The argument may be summarized thus:

1) The opening greeting in K, which is similar to that in B, but has no parallel in D.

[3] A. Faivre, "La documentation canonico-liturgique de l'église ancienne," *RevSR* 54 (1980), 204–219, 273–297, at 291–292.
[4] *Didascalia* 2.6.1, 2.1.5.

This, however, is simply a standard epistolary greeting and does not imply any direct dependence upon **B**.

> 2) In the statement of the love commandment **K** diverges from the version of **D**, the **K** version being comparable to the different version in **B**.

D	K	B
First you shall love the God who made you, your neighbour as yourself, and whatever you would not wish done to you, do not do to anyone else.	First you shall love the God who created you with all your heart and you shall glorify him who ransomed you from death. Such is the first commandment. The second: you shall love your neighbour as yourself. Such is the second commandment, on which the whole of the law and the prophets is dependent. Matthew said: Whatever you would not wish done to you, do to nobody else.	You shall love the one who created you, you shall fear the one who formed you, you shall glorify the one who ransomed you from death.

Whereas there is some similarity between **K** and **B** the two are not particularly close, and **K** and **D**, but not **B**, teach love for neighbour and the golden rule. Given that the context of the production and circulation of TWT is originally catechetical, the expansion of the saying making reference to the baptism by which the hearer is ransomed may be more widespread than simply these examples. It is indeed possible that this was in κ as well, even though it is not found in **E** (as this may be due to abbreviation in **E**.)

> 3) At **K**12 the commandment to treasure one's teacher is expanded in a manner with proximity to a similar statement at B.19.9.

D	K	B
My child, you shall remember both night and day remember the one who speaks to you the word of God.	Child, you shall love as the apple of your eye the one who speaks to you the word of God	You shall love everyone who speaks the word of the Lord to you as the apple of your eye

However, **E** also commands that the teacher be honoured "as the apple of an eye." The saying must therefore be in κ, and is not therefore the result of revision of TWT in the light of **B** but is part of a common tradition, perhaps deriving from Proverbs 7.2.

4) As has already been noted, there is a significant difference between **K** and **D** in the conclusion, for whereas **D** has a *Haustafel*, **K** has an eschatological conclusion with similarities with **B**.

K	B
We ask you, brethren, for as long as there is time, while you have amongst yourselves those for whom to labour, do not withhold anything that you possess. For the day of the Lord is near, on which all things will perish alongside the evil one. For the Lord will come and his reward with him. Be legislators for yourselves, be good counsellors for yourselves, taught of God. You shall guard what you have received, neither adding nor subtracting.	I ask you who are foremost, if you are willing to receive any advice from my positive awareness, keep with yourselves for whose good you may labour. Do not be wanting. The day is near on which all things will perish alongside the evil one. The Lord is near, as is his reward. I ask you again and again: Be good legislators for yourselves, remain faithful counsellors for yourselves, remove all hypocrisy from among you. May God, who has dominion over the entire world, grant you wisdom, understanding, perception, knowledge of his commands, patience. Be taught of God, seeking out what the Lord desires of you and so perform it that you may be found on the day of judgement.

Although there is some material in common here the two versions are not particularly close. Since **K** would appear to have been a relatively conservative redactor, on the basis of the manner in which the parallels to **E** are quite close, it would seem strange that he would be so radical in a revision of **B**. One may also question, if **K** possessed **B**, why, in view of the cosmologically dualist outlook betrayed elsewhere in **K**, he would omit the section concerning the angels set over the two ways. It therefore seems more likely that, as with the other supposed parallels to **B**, that this is a part of an independent and possibly oral tradition of which **K** is aware. In revising κ he saw fit to attribute the eschatological conclusion to the final speaker, omitting the *Haustafel* in order to make room for it. Nonetheless the proximity of these oral elements to **B** does enable us to label the tradition β, and to suggest that this was a source for **B**, just as it is an indirect source for **K**. There has not, however, been a wholesale revision of TWT undertaken by **K** with one eye on **B** and one on κ/δ, rather the redactor of **K**, whilst working with a written document, is aware of the tradition within a β form, and this awareness of the tradition has influenced his editing of the material. It may, indeed, be the redactor's awareness of the absence of the way of death from κ which leads to Peter's assertion that the Scriptures might teach of the "remaining exhortations."

This network of relationships may be expressed diagrammatically thus:

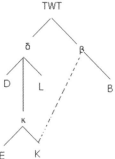

A long time has been spent on discussing what might be seen as a technical issue. However, the assertion that *K* had been in possession of *B* is so often found that some time had to be given to the refutation of this statement, and to making it clear both that the redactor of *K* was heir to a living tradition and that the redactor of *E* likewise came from a setting in which the Two Ways were still employed as a guide to those learning the way of Christ.

Translations

The summary of the commands of the apostles of catholic tradition

John said: "There are two ways, the one of life and the one of death; and there is great difference between the two.

Now that of life is this: First you shall love the God who made you with your whole heart. Second, you shall love your neighbour as yourself."

Matthew said: "Whatever you would not have happen to you, do not to any other. That is, do not do what you hate to another."

Peter said: "You shall not murder, you shall do no sin in your flesh, you shall not steal, you shall not practise sorcery, you shall not make potions, you shall not covet what is your neighbour's, you shall not swear falsely, you shall not bear false witness, you shall not speak evil, you shall not harbour evil, you shall not be double-minded or double-tongued. Your word shall not be empty, you shall not be grasping, nor rapacious nor hypocritical, nor malicious, nor arrogant. You shall not plot evil against your neighbour. You shall not hate any person, but some you shall rebuke, for some you shall pray, and some you shall love beyond your own life."

Andrew said: "Shun every bad person and all who are like them.[5] Do not be quick-tempered nor jealous nor quarrelsome nor furious, for these lead to murder."

[5]Or "bad thing."

Philip said: "Do not be given over to passion, for it leads to fornication."

Simon said: "Do not be a speaker of base words, nor immodestly curious. For from these adulteries come about."

James said: "Do not be an examiner of omens, not an enchanter, not an astrologer nor, so to speak, a lustrator, nor desire to know of or hear them. For from all of these idolatries come about."

Nathanael said: "Do not be a liar, nor a lover of money nor vainglorious. From all of these thefts come about. Do not be a grumbler, not impassioned, not self-willed nor evil-minded, for from all of these blasphemies come about. Be generous, since the generous shall inherit the Kingdom of God; be patient, merciful, a peacemaker, pure of heart, guileless, peaceable, good, preserving and fearing the words of God. Do not make yourself haughty, nor give your life over to presumption, do not let your life be spent with the exalted but with the righteous and lowly. Whatever befall you, accept these experiences as good, knowing that nothing occurs without God."

Thomas said: "Child, you shall love as the apple of your eye the one who speaks to you the word of God and is the cause of life to you and gives you the seal of the Lord. You shall remember him night and day, you shall honour him as a master. For inasmuch as Jesus Christ is discussed, the Lord is there. You shall seek him out, and the rest of the saints, so that you may find refreshment in their words. For in being cemented with the saints, a saint is sanctified. For the Lord through him has made you worthy to be given spiritual food and eternal life."

Kephas said: "You shall not make a schism, you shall make peace between those who are disputing, you shall judge justly, you shall not show partiality in rebuking anyone on account of a transgression, for there is equality with God. In your prayer you shall not be divided in your mind.

"If you have possessions as a result of your hands, give as a release for your sins. You shall not turn away a beggar. You shall share in common all things with your brothers, and you shall not claim anything as your own. For if you are companions in death, are you not much more so in mortal matters?"

Bartholomew said: "You shall not withdraw your hand from your son nor from your daughter, but yet from their youth you shall teach them the fear of the Lord. You shall confess your transgressions, You shall not forsake the commandments of the Lord, you shall not come to prayer with an evil conscience. You shall despise all hypocrisy, and everything that is not pleasing to the Lord. Let what you have received be preserved, neither adding nor detracting. This is the way of life."

The directions through Clement and the canons of the holy apostles[6]

Greetings, sons and daughters, in the name of the Lord Jesus Christ. John and Matthew and Peter and Andrew and Philip and Simon and James and Nathanael and Thomas and Kephas and Bartholomew and Jude the son of James.

1 In accordance with the command of Our Lord Jesus Christ the Saviour we gathered ourselves together, as he laid down for us: "Before you determine the eparchies, you are to calculate the numbers of the places,[7] the dignities of bishops, the seats of presbyters, the assistance offered by deacons, the understanding of readers, the blamelessness of widows and whatever is necessary for the foundation of the church, so that knowing the type of those things which are heavenly, they should guard themselves against every fault, seeing that, in the great day of judgement, they should give an account of those who heard and did not keep." And he ordered us to send these words out to the whole inhabited world.

[6]This version of the *Apostolic Church Order* (*K*) is based on my own text, which diverges significantly from previously published texts.

[7]This is to be taken as the number of episcopal seats, which are to be established before any provincial arrangements are made.

2   It seemed to us, therefore, that we should command you as an admonition of brotherhood and an exhortation, so that you might be mindful through the account of what the Lord revealed to each of us in accordance with the will of God through the Holy Spirit.

3   John said: "Brethren, since we know that we shall have to give an account of what was commanded us, let us not have regard for any person, but if someone should seem to say something which is improper, he should be contradicted." It seemed to all that John should speak first.

4   ₁John said: "There are two ways, the one of life and the one of death, and the difference between the two ways is great. ₂For the way of life is this. First you shall love the God who created you with all your heart and you shall glorify him who ransomed you from death. Such is the first commandment. ₃The second: you shall love your neighbour as yourself. Such is the second commandment, on which the whole of the law and the prophets is dependent."

5   Matthew said: "Whatever you would not wish done to you, do to nobody else. State the teaching of these maxims, brother Peter."

6   ₁Peter said: "You shall not murder, you shall not commit adultery, you shall not fornicate, you shall not despoil a child, you shall not steal, you shall not practise sorcery, you shall not make potions, you shall not destroy a child through abortion nor kill it once born, you shall not covet what is your neighbour's, ₂you shall not swear falsely, you shall not bear false witness, you shall not speak evil, you shall not harbour evil, you shall not be double-minded or double-tongued. For being double-tongued is a snare of death. Your word shall not be empty, nor false. ₃You shall not be grasping, nor rapacious, nor hypocritical, nor malicious, nor arrogant. You shall not plot evil against your neighbour. You shall not hate any person, but some you shall rebuke, some you shall pity, for some you shall pray, and some you shall love more than your own life."

7   Andrew said: "My child, shun every evil person and all who are like to him. Do not be quick-tempered, for anger leads to murder. For rage is a male demon. Do not be jealous or quarrelsome or ragingly aggressive. For murder is begotten from these."

8   ₁Philip said: "My child, do not be given over to passion. For lust leads to fornication and drags people towards itself. For lust is a female demon, and one with anger, the other with pleasure, destroys those who go close to them. ₂The way of an evil spirit is a soul's sin, and when it has a narrow place of entry in somebody it expands itself and leads that soul on to all evil things, and does not allow the person to look out and see the truth. ₃Let your rage be measured and rein it in and bring it to a halt in a short distance, so that it cannot lead you to an evil deed. ₄For rage and evil pleasure, when they remain a long time, gain strength to become demons, and when a person yields to them they swell up in his soul and become greater and lead him on to unjust deeds and they mock him and take pleasure in the person's destruction."

9   Simon said: "Child, do not be a speaker of base words, nor immodestly curious. For from these adulteries come about."

10   James said: "My child, do not be an examiner of omens, since this leads to idolatry, nor an enchanter nor an astrologer nor a lustrator, nor desire to see or hear these things. For from all of these are idolatries begotten."

11   ₁Nathanael said: "My child, do not be a liar, since falsehood leads to theft, nor a lover of money nor vainglorious. For from all of these are thefts begotten. ₂My child, do not be a grumbler, since it leads to blasphemy, nor self-willed nor evil-minded. For from all of these are blasphemies begotten.₃Be generous, for the generous will inherit the Kingdom of the Heavens. ₄Be patient, merciful, a peace-maker, pure in heart from every evil, guileless and peaceable, good and guarding and fearing the words which you heard. ₅Do not make yourself haughty, nor commit your life to the exalted, but associate with the righteous and lowly. 6 Whatever befall you, accept these experiences as good, knowing that nothing occurs without God."

12   ₁Thomas said: "Child, you shall love as the apple of your eye the one who speaks to you the word of God and is the cause of life to you and gives you the seal of the Lord. You shall remember him night and day, you shall honour him as the Lord. For inasmuch as the dominion is discussed, the Lord is there. ₂You shall daily seek out his face, as well as the rest of the saints, so that you may find refreshment in their words. For in being cemented with the saints you shall be sanctified as a saint. ₃You shall honour him as much as you are able from your sweat and from the labour of your hands. If the Lord through him has made you worthy to be given spiritual food and drink and eternal life, much the more should you bring him corruptible and temporary food. 'For the workman is worthy of his hire' (Luke 10.7; 1 Tim 5.18) and 'You shall not muzzle a threshing ox' (Deut 25.4; 1 Tim 5.18) and 'Nobody plants a vine and does not eat of its fruit.'" (1 Cor 9.7, 9)

13   ₁Kephas said: "You shall not make schisms, you shall make peace between those who are disputing, you shall judge justly, you shall not show partiality in rebuking any transgression, for wealth does not count before the Lord. Status does not impress nor does beauty give advantage, for before him all are equal. ₂In your prayer you shall not be divided in your mind, whether it will be or not. ₃Do not be one who stretches out hands to take, whilst retracting them to avoid giving. If you have gained through your hands, you shall give a ransom for your sins. Do not hesitate to give, nor grumble in your giving, for you know who is the good dispenser of rewards. ₄You shall not turn away a beggar. You shall have all things in common with your brother, and you shall not claim anything as your own. For if you are companions in immortality, are you not much more so in what is corruptible?"

14 ₁Bartholomew said: "We ask you, brethren, for as long as there is time, while you have amongst yourselves those for whom to labour, do not withhold anything that you possess. ₂For the day of the Lord is near, on which all things will perish alongside the evil one. For the Lord will come and his reward with him. ₃Be legislators for yourselves, be good counsellors for yourselves, taught of God. You shall guard what you have received, neither adding nor subtracting."

15 Peter said: "Brothers, the Scriptures will teach of the remaining exhortations. But let us draw up in order what we have commanded." All said: "Let Peter speak."

16 ₁Peter said: "If there should occur a shortage of men, and there are insufficient competent to elect to the episcopate from among twelve, they should write to the neighbouring churches, where one is established, so that three selected men might come from there carefully to determine which is worthy, whether any has a good reputation among the heathen, (1 Tim 3.7) being without fault, (Cf. 1 Tim 3.2) whether a friend of the poor, whether temperate, not a drunkard, (Cf. Titus 1.8; 1 Tim 3.2) not a fornicator, not grasping or abusive, or a respecter of persons or anything of that nature. ₂It is good should he be unmarried, otherwise he should be of one wife, having some education, and able to interpret the Scriptures, even if he is unlettered. He should be generous and overflowing with love for all, so that a bishop should not come under accusation on any account by the many."

17 ₁John said: "The bishop who has been installed, knowing the care and the love of God of those who are with him, should install two presbyters of whom he approves." ₂All said in reply: "Not two but three. For there are twenty-four presbyters, twelve on the right and twelve on the left."

18 ₁John said: "You have recalled this well, brothers. For those on the right receive the phials from the archangels and bear them to the master, and those on the left have authority over the company of angels. (Rev 4.4,8) ₂Therefore the presbyters should have been a long time in the world, having kept themselves from congress with women in their lives, generous towards the brotherhood, not respecters of persons, struggling alongside the bishop and participating in the mysteries together with him, gathering the people and devoted to the pastor ₃The presbyters on the right are to assist those who oversee the altar, so that they may distribute the gifts of honour and receive them as necessary. The presbyters on the left are to assist the congregation, so that it may be peaceful and without disturbance, once it has been instructed in all submission ₄But if anyone who has been warned should respond rashly, those at the altar, acting in concert, should pronounce a like decision, as is deserved, so that the rest might be in fear, and so that they do not accept any person, and so that the evil might not spread further like a cancer and all be infected."

19 James said: "A reader should be appointed after careful testing. He should not be a babbler, or a drunkard, or a jester. He should be of upstanding life, submissive, well-intentioned, taking the lead in the assemblies on the Lord's days, who is good to listen to and is able to construct a narrative, aware that he labours in the place of an evangelist. (2 Tim 4.5) For whoever fills the ears of the ignorant shall be reckoned as written before God."

20 ₁Matthew said: "Three deacons should be appointed. It is written: 'Every matter of the Lord shall be established by three.' (Deut 19.15; Matt 18.16; 2 Cor 8.1.) ₂They should be proved in every ministry, with witness borne by the congregation, married once, (1 Tim 3.12) educating their children (1 Tim 3.12), temperate, (1 Tim 3.2) fair, (1 Tim 3.3) peaceable, not grumblers, not double-tongued, not irascible, (Titus 1.7) for anger distracts a reasonable man, (Prov 15.1) who neither accept the persons of the rich nor oppress the poor, not given to much use of wine, (1 Tim 3.8) intelligent, ₃good at exhorting to secret works, as they oblige the brothers who have possessions to open their hands, and themselves generous, communicative, honoured by the congregation with all honour, esteem and fear, carefully mindful of those who are conducting themselves in a disorderly manner, warning some, encouraging others, threatening others, but leaving the scoffers entirely alone, mindful that those opposed to reason, the scoffers and the abusive have resisted Christ."

21 ₁Kephas said: "Three widows should be appointed. Two are to continue in prayer for all who are in temptation and for revelations concerning whatever is necessary. ₂One is to assist women who are being troubled by sickness. She is to be a good minister, discreet in communicating what is necessary to the presbyters, not avaricious, not fond of much wine, so that she may be sober in her service during the night, and in whatever other acts of charity she desires to perform. These foremost treasures of the Lord are good."

22 ₁Andrew said: "Deacons perform noble deeds; they go around everywhere, night and day, neither looking down upon the poor or paying undue attention to the wealthy, recognizing any who is oppressed and not excluding him from the collections, ₂obliging those who are able to put something aside for good works, having in mind the words of our teacher: 'You saw me hungry, and fed me not.' Those who serve nobly and blamelessly set aside for themselves the position of the pastorate."

23 ₁Philip said: "The layman should be content to concern himself with matters pertaining to the laity, submitting to whose who attend to the altar. ₂Each should please God in his own position, not striving with each other in the matter of rank, each in that to which he was called and is placed by Christ. ₃None should obstruct the path of another, for neither do the angels anything contrary to their station, or take another's route."

24 Andrew said: "It would be useful, brothers, to establish ministries for the women."

25 Peter said: "We have previously legislated. Let us carefully explain regarding the offering of the body and the blood."

26 John said: "You are forgetting, brothers, that when the teacher requested the bread and the cup and blessed them saying: 'This is my Body and Blood,' he did not permit the women to stand alongside us. Martha said it was on account of Mary because he saw her smiling. Mary said: 'I did not laugh at this. Previously he said to us, when he was teaching, that the weak would be saved through the strong.'"

27 Kephas said: "Some things should be remembered: that women should not pray upright but seated on the ground."[8]

28 James said: "How then can we establish ministries for the women, except the ministry of supporting women in need?"

29 Philip said: "This, brothers, concerning sharing: whoever does a deed gathers for himself a good treasury. Whoever gathers treasure in the Kingdom is reckoned an enrolled labourer by God."

---

[8] There is ample evidence of women praying in a standing position. I argue in *Apostolic Church Order* that this is in order to avoid women manifesting ecstatic behaviour in prophesying.

30 Peter said: "Brothers, we do not command these things as those who have the power to compel, but as having a command from the Lord. We ask you to keep the commandments, neither detracting from them nor adding, in the name of Our Lord, to whom be glory for ever. Amen."

A synoptic table of the way of life in K and E

K	E
John said: "There are two ways, the one of life and the one of death, and the difference between the two ways is great. For the way of life is this. First you shall love the God who created you with all your heart and you shall glorify him who ransomed you from death. Such is the first commandment. The second: you shall love your neighbour as yourself. Such is the second commandment, on which the whole of the law and the prophets is dependent."	John said: "There are two ways, the one of life and the one of death; and there is great difference between the two. Now that of life is this: First you shall love the God who made you with your whole heart.
	Second, you shall love your neighbour as yourself."
Matthew said: "Whatever you would not wish done to you, do to nobody else. State the teaching of these maxims, brother Peter."	Matthew said: "Whatever you would not have happen to you, do not to any other. That is, do not do what you hate to another."
Peter said: "You shall not murder, you shall not commit adultery, you shall not fornicate, you shall not despoil a child, you shall not steal, you shall not practise sorcery, you shall not make potions, you shall not destroy a child through abortion nor kill it once born, you shall not covet what is your neighbour's, you shall not swear falsely, you shall not bear false witness, you shall not speak evil, you shall not harbour evil, you shall not be double-minded or double-tongued. For being double-tongued is a snare of death. Your word shall not be empty, nor false. You shall not be grasping, nor rapacious, nor	Peter said: "You shall not murder, you shall do no sin in your flesh, you shall not steal, you shall not practise sorcery, you shall not make potions, you shall not covet what is your neighbour's, you shall not swear falsely, you shall not bear false witness, you shall not speak evil, you shall not harbour evil, you shall not be double-minded or double-tongued. Your word shall not be empty, you shall not be grasping, nor rapacious nor

K	E
hypocritical, nor malicious, nor arrogant. You shall not plot evil against your neighbour. You shall not hate any person, but some you shall rebuke, some you shall pity, for some you shall pray, and some you shall love more than your own life." Andrew said: "My child, shun every evil person and all who are like to him. Do not be quick-tempered, for anger leads to murder. For rage is a male demon. Do not be jealous or quarrelsome or ragingly aggressive. For murder is begotten from these."	hypocritical, nor malicious, nor arrogant. You shall not plot evil against your neighbour. You shall not hate any person, but some you shall rebuke, for some you shall pray, and some you shall love beyond your own life." Andrew said: "Shun every bad person and all who are like them. Do not be quick-tempered nor
	jealous nor quarrelsome nor furious, for these lead to murder."
Philip said: "My child, do not be given over to passion. For lust leads to fornication and drags people towards itself. For lust is a female demon, and one with anger, the other with pleasure, destroys those who go close to them. The way of an evil spirit is a soul's sin, and when it has a narrow place of entry in somebody it expands itself and leads that soul on to all evil things, and does not allow the person to look out and see the truth. Let your rage be measured and rein it in and bring it to a halt in a short distance, so that it cannot lead you to an evil deed. For rage and evil pleasure, when they remain a long time, ˙ gain strength to become demons, and when a person yields to them they swell up in his soul and become greater and lead him on to unjust deeds and they mock him and take pleasure in the person's destruction."	Philip said: "Do not be given over to passion, for it leads to fornication."
Simon said: "Child, do not be a speaker of base words, nor immodestly curious. For from these adulteries come about." James said: "My child, do not be an examiner of omens, since this leads to idolatry, nor an enchanter nor an astrologer nor a lustrator, nor desire to see or hear these things. For from all of these are idolatries begotten."	Simon said: "Do not be a speaker of base words, nor immodestly curious. For from these adulteries come about." James said: "Do not be an examiner of omens, not an enchanter not an astrologer nor, so to speak, a lustrator, nor desire to know of or hear them. For from all of these idolatries come about."

K	E

Nathanael said: "My child, do not be a liar, since falsehood leads to theft, nor a lover of money nor vainglorious. For from all of these are thefts begotten. ₂My child, do not be a grumbler, since it leads to blasphemy, nor self-willed nor evil-minded. For from all of these are blasphemies begotten. Be generous, for the generous will inherit the Kingdom of the Heavens. Be patient, merciful, a peacemaker, purei n heart from every evil, guileless and peaceable, good and guarding and fearing the words which you heard. Do not make yourself haughty,

nor commit your life to the exalted, but associate with the righteous and lowly. Whatever befall you, accept these experiences as good, knowing that nothing occurs without God." Thomas said: "Child, you shall love as the apple of your eye the one who speaks to you the word of God and is the cause of life to you and gives you the seal of the Lord. You shall remember him night and day, you shall honour him as the Lord. For inasmuch as the dominion is discussed, the Lord is there. You shall daily seek out his face, as well as the rest of the saints, so that you may find refreshment in their words. For in being cemented with the saints you shall be sanctified as a saint. You shall honour him as much as you are able from your sweat and from the labour of your hands. If the Lord through him has made you worthy to be given spiritual food and drink and eternal life, much the more should you bring him corruptible and temporary food. 'For the workman is worthy of his hire' and 'You shall not muzzle a threshing ox' and 'Nobody plants a vine and does not eat of its fruit.'" Kephas said: "You shall not make schisms, you shall make peace between

Nathanael said: "Do not be a liar, nor a lover of money nor vainglorious. From all of these thefts come about.   Do not be a grumbler, not impassioned, not self-willed nor evil-minded, for from all of these blasphemies come about. Be generous, since the generous shall inherit the Kingdom of God; be patient, merciful, a peacemaker, pure of heart,   guileless, peaceable, good, preserving and fearing the words of God. Do not make yourself haughty, nor give your life over to presumption, do not let your life be spent with the exalted but with the righteous and lowly. Whatever befall you, accept these experiences as good, knowing that nothing occurs without God." Thomas said: "Child, you shall love as the apple of your eye the one who speaks to you the word of God and is the cause of life to you and gives you the seal of the Lord. You shall remember him night and day, you shall honour him as a master. For inasmuch as Jesus Christ is discussed, the Lord is there. You shall seek him out, and the rest of the saints, so that you may find refreshment in their words. For in being cemented with the saints a saint is sanctified.

For the Lord through him has made you worthy to be given spiritual food and eternal life."

Kephas said: "You shall not make a schism, you shall make peace between

K	E

those who are disputing, you shall judge justly, you shall not show partiality in rebuking any transgression, for wealth does not count before the Lord. Status does not impress nor does beauty give advantage, for before him all are equal. In your prayer you shall not be divided in your mind, whether it will be or not. Do not be one who stretches out hands to take, whilst retracting them to avoid giving. If you have gained through your hands, you shall give a ransom for your sins. Do not hesitate to give, nor grumble in your giving, for you know who is the good dispenser of rewards. You shall not turn away a beggar. You shall have all things in common with your brother, and you shall not claim anything as your own. For if you are companions in immortality, are you not much more so in what is corruptible?" Bartholomew said: "We ask you, brethren, for as long as there is time, while you have amongst yourselves those for whom to labour, do not withhold anything that you possess. For the day of the Lord is near, on which all things will perish alongside the evil one. For the Lord will come and his reward with him. Be legislators for yourselves, be good counsellors for yourselves, taught of God. You shall guard what you have received, neither adding nor subtracting."	those who are disputing, you shall judge justly, you shall not show partiality in rebuking anyone on account of a transgression,
	
	                                                for there is equality with God. In your prayer you shall not be divided in your mind.
	
	                                          If you have possessions as a result of your hands, give as a release for your sins.
	
	                                  You shall not turn away a beggar. You shall share in common all things with your brothers, and you shall not claim anything as your own. For if you are companions in death, are you not much more so in mortal matters?" Bartholomew said: "You shall not withdraw your hand from your son nor from your daughter, but yet from their youth you shall teach them the fear of The Lord. You shall confess your transgressions, You shall not forsake the commandments of the Lord, you shall not come to prayer with an evil conscience. You shall despise all hypocrisy, and everything that is not pleasing to the Lord. Let what you have received be preserved, neither adding nor detracting. This is the way of life."

CHAPTER FOUR

The Two Ways in the monastic tradition

Before Christianity became the official religion of the Roman Empire early in the fourth century, individuals had embraced ascetic practices and had sought solitude with God in the deserts. However in the post-Constantinian period this practice became more organized and extensive, possibly as a protest against the conformity of the church to the Empire, possibly as a substitute for martyrdom in a more intense attempt to live out the baptismal covenant, or possibly simply because under conditions of peace it was possible for the movement to be organized and so to flourish. Thus in the fourth century and onward there are growing numbers of monks organized into communities. In this period the TWT finds its way into the rules by which these communities were organized and by which the monk was challenged to a more complete following of the Gospel.

The (Egyptian) *Canons of Hippolytus*, probably from the third century, conclude with a canon concerning baptism and the Pascha, which seems to include some kind of post-baptismal discourse as the canon turns to direct speech. The discourse starts out by describing the state of those who, having renounced sin, fall back into evil ways, and then outlines the duties of a Christian. In this part there is perhaps some influence of the TWT, for instance in the statement that a Christian should not have "two measures" in giving and receiving, in stating that a Christian should not be a grumbler, in exhorting the Christian to treat his slaves as his own children. These are the duties of all Christians, but subsequently the discourse goes on to say: "If the Christian desires to be of angelic rank let him keep away from women completely . . ." which leads in turn to a description of a way of life which approaches the monastic ideal, and to a homily on the temptations of Jesus in the desert. We may see that as a greater ideal of perfection than that realizable by the Christian in the world is coming about, this is joined to a more basic statement of Christian duties. It is the same phenomenon which we meet in these monastic documents, and most particularly in the pseudo-Athanasian texts given below, where a basic statement of Christian practice is followed by rules of conduct for the monastic life. As in the other two writings in this chapter, namely the *Life of Shenoute* and the *Rule of St Benedict*, the basic instructions of TWT are subsumed into monastic rules. This has, we may surmise, come about through circulation of TWT teaching as the basic instruction of the baptized; given that the monastic ideal is the perfect living out of the baptismal covenant and the maintenance of baptismal purity, it is entirely reasonable to see how the two grow together. It is also possible that the influence of the tradition as a standard for clergy influenced its use as a standard for monastics likewise. Rordorf states that in becoming part of the monastic rule itself (in the sixth century, he states, which may well be right) the TWT had ceased to exist,[1] but we may suggest, in the light of the mediaeval survivals noted in our final chapter, that this is simply a literary accident. The tradition is preserved in writing in monastic rules but clearly survived in the west at least as the basis for the conduct of all Christians, in which context we may see the work of Lactantius.[2]

[1]W. Rordorf, "An Aspect of the Judeo-Christian Ethic, 148–164 at 163.

[2]In the sixth book of the *Divine Institutes*, an apologetic work attempting to commend Christianity to the educated elite of the day, Lactantius, a Christian rhetorician of the fourth century, sets out a version of the two ways. "The ways by which human life must proceed are two, one which tends towards heaven, the other which drags down to hell. Poets have introduced them in their poems and philosophers in their disputations. Philosophers indeed have identified one as of the virtues, the other of the vices, and that which is to be assigned to virtues is at first approach said to be hard and rugged. Anyone who attains to its summit by overcoming great difficulty should thereafter have a level path, a light and pleasant plain in which to gather the

Nonetheless the rise of monasticism was a means by which the covenantal basis of the tradition was renewed and sustained in the west and the east alike; indeed, we may note that the relationship between Shenoute and his monks was the covenant which they formed.

There are three sets of documents within this collection, a version of TWT from the Arabic *Life of Shenoute*, a pair of related versions contained in monastic instructions attributed to Athanasius, and a section of the *Rule of Saint Benedict*.

PART ONE: THE LIFE OF SHENOUTE

Introduction

Shenoute was a leading figure in Egyptian monasticism through much of the fifth century. *The Life of Shenoute* is attributed to Besa, Shenoute's successor, and was written in Coptic; the Arabic transla-

---

abundant and delightful fruits of all his labours, whereas those who have been put off by the difficulty of the first approach slip and slide away into the way of vices which at its first entrance has the appearance of being pleasant and far-better trod, and then, when they have proceeded slightly further along it, find its pleasant nature suddenly withdrawn and a steep path arising, now strewn with stones and then obstructed with thorns, then interposed with deep cataracts or violent torrents, so that they have to struggle, hesitate, slip and fall." (*Divine Institutes*, 6.3) As even this brief citation shows, this is a very remote relation to the tradition and the hand of Lactantius himself lies heavily upon it. Nonetheless, insofar as Lactantius' work is intended for conversion we may see that there is some connection with the catechetical purpose of the tradition. The difference is that the catechetical versions are intended for internal ecclesial use whereas Lactantius addresses himself from within the church to the world outside, and dresses his work in a manner likely to appeal to the educated pagan. Although there is a degree of divergence from the tradition we should moreover note the suggestion of G. Kendeffy that the idea of the two ways lies deep in Lactantius' thought. (A paper entitled "Lactantius and the two ways" is forthcoming in *Studia patristica*; I am most grateful to Prof. Kendeffy for sharing his work with me.) It is, moreover, possible that Lactantius has the tradition from the eastern empire as, although he was born in Africa, he taught rhetoric in Bithynia, from which post he was dismissed on the grounds of his Christianity.

tion is considerably later. The section containing two-ways material does not appear in the Coptic version of the *Life* and may therefore be seen to have been an interpolation, but nonetheless the inclusion of the material indicates that the tradition was still in circulation in monastic circles. Indeed it is quite likely that this interpolation is derived from a Coptic source. The order of the two ways is close to that of *D*, but the absence of the Gospel section indicates in turn that this was a version of the δ strand, but not *D* itself.

Translation (by Posy Clayton)

He (Shenoute) always used to teach us that the way was easy. The way is a double one, one leading to life and the other to death with a huge difference between the two. The way to life is this: before all else, love the Lord your God with all your heart, with all your soul and with every thought. Love your neighbour as yourself in all your thinking.

Whatever you would not wish done to you, do not do to anyone else. So act thus. These are the deeds (to be observed) one by one with the first of them being, do not kill, do not fornicate, do not make yourself impure by loving impurity, do not act sinfully, do not steal, do not practise sorcery, do not bring about an abortion for a pregnant woman through a potion and do not kill her newborn, do not covet the goods of your friend and your relative, do not break an oath, do not speak falsely, do not speak evil of anyone lest the Lord grow angry with you. Do not be changeable, do not speak false or empty words, do not hold back anything from a labourer's wage lest he seek help from the Lord and is heard by Him as the Lord Jesus the Messiah is not far from us. My child, do not take by force, do not loot or be a usurer or wickedly disavow (a debt). My child, do not be proud, for the proud man is detested by God. Do not speak ill of your friend, your relative or your rival, for if you act thus God will love him more than you. My child, do not hate any person for they are the image and likeness of God. If somebody slips and takes a false step falling into sin, reprimand him among yourselves alone as other kinsfolk have done and love him as yourself. Flee from every evil, do not associate with him who does bad things lest your life be reduced and you die before your allotted time. My child, do not be envious or jealous, do not mislead, for these teach man to kill. My child, do not let your zeal be for lust as lust leads to adultery. My child, do not utter obscene words, do not have covetous eyes for they make false witness. My child, do not ask, 'what is it?' or 'why is it?', for (questioning) leads to the worship of idols. Do not count the hours for unhappiness, sighing, anxiety and fear fall on those who act thus. My child, do not receive incanters and magicians hospitably and do not approach them or have conversation with them, for any man who frequents them does not draw near to God. My child, do not be a liar, for falsehood leads to theft. My child, do not be a lover of silver, do not boast, for from these is born the desire to kill. My child, do not grumble, for grumbling leads to blasphemy. My child, do not be small-minded, do not think with evil intent but be gentle, for the gentle inherit the earth. My child, be patient, long-suffering, merciful, simple-hearted and faithful in all actions: be good, always fearful and trembling before the words and commands of God. Do not be proud-hearted but always modest. Do not grow close to the rich but associate with people who are devout and humble, for the prophet David owed his salvation to humility many times. Whenever good or evil happen to you, receive it with gratitude for you know that nothing happens to you without the will of God, your God. My child, remember the word of God within your heart, night and day, for the Lord is present wherever anyone mentions his name and He is eternally worthy of respect and praise. My child, follow the path of purity at all times to become strong and powerful in its excellent system and enjoy its sweet words and delightful tales. My child, do not seek discord or argument among your fellow men but seek to make peace among those in disagreement. Then judge with justice and do not be embarrassed to reprimand the criminal for his faults or the sinner for his sin. My child, do not open your hand to receive nor close it to avoid giving. Be careful to act as long as you are able, giving to the poor in exchange for your many sins. Indeed, do not be changeable when you give and if you give do not be saddened nor be regretful if you act mercifully. You might well know that it is Jesus the Messiah who pardons sins and recompenses the honest and the faithful man. My child, do not turn your face from the poor but give according to your power. Share with all who are troubled and in need, for if we share our perishable goods with the disenfranchised we shall share with them in goods which are lasting and eternal. If we follow these recommendations we may travel along the road of life and the blessed path to eternity which belongs to the one king, the Lord Jesus the Messiah who is generous to those who desire him.

As to the way of death, whoever follows its track and walks in its paths shall die the death of a bad man because of all its evil deeds which are: cursing, murder, pillage, violence, hypocrisy and every bad deed. Have we not explained it (all) lest someone be led astray and fall in the road of death and travel its paths to bad deeds for the man untried in such things grows proud.

This is the teaching which our holy father, Anba Shenoute, always used to teach us on every occasion and it is this, our children, we have explained to you at this time.

Part two: the pseudo-Athanasian material

Introduction

The second manifestation of the TWT from the monastic tradition is represented by two clearly related documents, the *Syntagma doctrinae* and the *Fides patrum*. Both are attributed, erroneously, to Athanasius.

The *Syntagma*, as may readily be seen, is a set of instructions addressed to monks; however, certain elements of TWT appear set within these instructions, first, in a manner reminiscent of the conclusion of *Canons of Hippolytus*, in the statement at the beginning of the major commandments, and further in the course of the instructions.

The *Fides patrum* has similar contents to the *Syntagma* and is in many places very closely parallel, but it is prefaced by a version of the Nicene creed and various anathemas attached thereto. However, its conclusion does not include some material found within the *Syntagma*. There is also a Coptic version of this material as part of a collection extant in two MSS which comprises a version of the creed with the signatures of the bishops and with anathemas, the monastic section which we recognize from the Greek, and a further ethical document having many echoes of the Church order tradition.[3]

Given the proximity of the three we must discuss the relationship obtaining between them.

As discussed in the previous chapter, we may determine the relationship between three similar documents by first discovering which of the three is the middle term. If the three versions are arranged in parallel columns one finds that whereas *Fides patrum* and *Syntagma* are frequently in agreement, and differ significantly from the Coptic, there are nonetheless points in which the Coptic is in agreement with *Fides patrum* and not with *Syntagma*. A few examples may suffice.

Syntagma	Coptic	*Fides patrum*
Do not make yourself naked in front of anyone, apart from the necessity of washing in sickness brought about through great weakness.	Do not make yourself naked in a bath nor before any person without necessity, such as, for example, in sickness or in great need, in water	Do not make yourself naked in front of anyone, except in necessity, in washing or in sickness, or when in need of the waters.

[3]Edited by Eugène Revillout, *Le concile de Nicée d'après les textes coptes et les diverses collections canoniques* (Paris: Imprimerie nationale, 1881), 25–57.

Syntagma	**Coptic**	*Fides patrum*
Do not keep sabbaths.	Do not keep the sabbath, like the Jews.	Do not observe sabbaths as do the Jews.

Syntagma	**Coptic**	*Fides patrum*
Do not omit a fast, that is to say Wednesday and Friday	Do not omit any fast of the Lord, that is of Wednesday or Friday	Do not omit the fast of the Lord, that is to say Wednesday and Friday

Syntagma	**Coptic**	*Fides patrum*
Do not be money-loving, nor sordidly greedy, nor a lover of material goods, nor a lover of wealth. For they who are such cannot be pleasing to God.	Do not be money-loving, do not gather wealth for yourself. Do not seek to obtain gold or silver, but only what is necessary for food and clothing. The friends of mammon, or those who are its servants, do not know how to please God.	Do not be money-loving, nor sordidly greedy, nor super-wealthy, Do not desire to gain silver or gold, except only as a means of obtaining food and clothing. For the friends of mammon cannot also be pleasing as servants to God.

Syntagma	**Coptic**	*Fides patrum*
You should not fast on sabbath or Sunday.	Do not fast on the sabbath for the whole day. For it is not proper to fast on a sabbath until the evening, but only until the sixth or seventh hour, for the setting of the sun is the beginning of the Sunday.	Do not fast on the sabbath for the whole day, for it is improper that you should fast the whole day on the sabbath until the setting of the sun, that is until the sixth or the seventh hour. The sun should not set upon you while you fast, as Sunday is coming on.

As such we may say that *Fides patrum* is the middle term as it generally agrees with *Sytagma* against the Coptic though occasionally it agrees with the Coptic against the *Syntagma*.

There are, however, two points at which the Coptic clearly agrees with *Syntagma* against *Fides patrum*.

Syntagma	Coptic	*Fides patrum*
. . . but have it hidden within. Neither should you wrap yourself in skins	. . . but that it is hidden within. Do not dress yourself in a skin	. . . but have it hidden within,
lest somehow you receive human glory. . . .	lest you receive human glory	lest you receive human glory . . .

This, however, can be explained by suggesting scribal error, namely that the scribe of *Fides patrum* missed the reference to skins and went on to the final clause.

The second point of agreement between the Coptic and the *Syntagma* against *Fides patrum* is to be found in the conclusions: that of *Fides patrum* concludes with directions which are to be addressed to women, whereas *Syntagma* and the Coptic version go on to discuss catechumens briefly, and then to discuss proper persons from whom offerings are to be received. This, likewise, can be explained through reference to the scribal process. One may suggest, given that *Fides patrum* is extant in a single manuscript, that the exemplar had lost its last page and a conclusion was subsequently added by a scribe, who was aware that his copy was defective. Thus in the translation which follows the short ending is given, followed by a longer ending supplied from the Coptic version; there is a close relationship between *Fides patrum* and the Coptic version, and so the Coptic may give us an idea of the contents of the missing conclusion.

If *Fides patrum* is the middle term between the versions the following relationships are possible.

a: *Fides patrum* was created by combining the *Syntagma* with the Coptic version.

b: *Fides patrum* is derived from the *Syntagma* and the Coptic version was translated in turn from *Fides patrum*.

c: *Fides patrum* is a rendition of a Coptic original, from which *Syntagma* was in turn derived.

d: Both the Coptic and the *Fides patrum* are versions of the *Syntagma*.

No other set of relationships is possible, unless further hypothetical documents are unnecessarily brought into play.[4] A detailed discussion is beyond the scope of this book, but I would suggest that the least likely arrangement is the first. This would be a bizarre proceeding, and is only mentioned as it is a theoretical possibility.

There is no clear way of determining which of the other possible relationships might obtain. However, there are two aspects which give me cause to consider that the Coptic version is a translation of *Fides patrum*.[5] Firstly, the Coptic version is part of a collection including other material; I am therefore inclined to the view that the author of *Fides patrum* would not have excerpted this material from a collection, whereas the Coptic translator might have included it as part of a collection. Secondly, there is one point where it seems that the Coptic translator has misunderstood the point of a statement:

Syntagma	Coptic	*Fides patrum*
Be moderate in clothing, not using soft clothes, not with your clothing appearing to be the dress of the righteous, that is not going about in rags.	Pay attention to the manner in which you wear your clothes, not wearing splendid or delicate clothes, but dress yourself in the clothes of the pure, that is to say, do not go about in rags.	Be moderate in clothing, not using soft clothes, not appearing to be righteous in your clothing, that is not going about in rags.

[4]P. Battifol, *Syntagma doctrinae* (Studia patristica 2; Paris: Ernest Leroux, 1890), 135, presents an extraordinarily and unnecessarily complex genealogy by which the *Syntagma* and a hypothetical document (y) are each derived from a prior hypothetical document (x), and the *Fides patrum* and the Coptic version are each derived from y.

[5]P. Battifol, *Didascalia CCCXVIII patrum* (Paris: Ernest Leroux, 1887), in a note appended to his text, suggested that *Fides patrum* had been translated from Coptic, but by the time he came to edit *Syntagma doctrinae* in 1890, had changed his mind.

Thus if the Coptic version is a translation of the *Fides patrum*, two possibilities remain, namely that the *Fides patrum* is a reworking of the *Syntagma*, from which the Coptic version was in turn derived, or that both the Coptic version and the *Syntagma* are independent versions of *Fides patrum*.

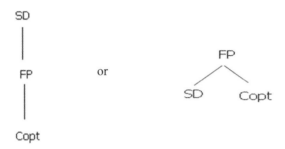

If one were to see the *Syntagma* as a reworking of the *Fides patrum* one would have to account for the omission of the credal material by the redactor of the *Syntagma*. It is difficult to see why this, and any attribution to the fathers of Nicaea, should be removed. Thus it seems most probable, though far from certain, that *Syntagma* is the first document in the series, and that *Fides patrum* reworked it.

Revillout had suggested that the material collected in the Coptic versions was derived from the Council of Alexandria in 362; Batiffol, however, points out that there is no reflection in the collection of materials of the key decisions of that council, namely the penalization of bishops who had failed when persecuted by Constantius, the anathematization of Eunomius and Macedonius, and the agreement of the equivalence of the Greek term hypostasis and the Latin term persona to refer to the persons of the Trinity, in the creed found in the *Fides patrum*.[6] Significant in that creed and

---

[6]Battifol, *Syntagma*, 135–138, in response to the work of Revillout cited above.

its anathemas, however, are the discussion of anthropomorphism, and the implied condemnation of Apollinarius in the statement that Christ was ". . . truly body and soul and not in appearance, for thus he wished perfectly to save humanity." These would each place the creed in the latter part of the fourth century. Battifol also notes the relative simplicity of the statements regarding the Holy Spirit, and suggests therefore that this precedes Constantinople, but we may note nonetheless that the *homoousion* of the Spirit is affirmed, and so we should not be so precise as Battifol, who places this between 375 and 381. Nonetheless, the debate about anthropomorphism was very current in the monastic communities of Egypt, to which this nest of documents must be attributed, and spilled over in 399 into the Origenist controversy; those who denied anthropomorphism were charged with following Origen in various heresies. The absence of a mention of Origen in this context or of any anathema on "Origenist" opinions suggests therefore that this preceded the end of the fourth century, whilst enmeshed in the controversies which marked the last quarter of that century.

Batiffol then considers the non-credal material, and notes a great deal of similarity between the disciplinary statements about having women living with the continents, about dress, about food and inns, and the conduct of business, and the various disciplinary canons of the councils of the fourth century. He also notes that this is the period in which the coenobitism which the *Syntagma* regulates grew up, but during which a class of continents living in the world, whose existence is assumed by the *Syntagma*, continued to exist, and finally he notes close similarities between this monastic rule and the directions with which Epiphanius' *Medicine Chest* concludes, suggesting that Epiphanius was dependent on a document much like the *Syntagma*. All of this tends to point to a date in the third quarter of the fourth century. I would not disagree with any of this assessment. If this is the date for the *Syntagma*, and if *Syntagma* is the first document in the series, then the *Fides patrum* is nonetheless not much later since it was probably completed before the end of the fourth century. If, however, *Fides patrum* is the prior document then it is not clear when the *Syntagma* was produced.

Elements of the TWT are not hard to discern within these works, even though the completed works are a world away from the address to the catechumens of the *Didache*. The order of topics makes it clear that the TWT source is a branch of the δ tradition, though the absence of the Gospel section indicates that it is not *D* itself,[7] and the absence of any apostolic attribution indicates that it is not κ either. In line with our suggestion above, Batiffol suggests that the monastic work has been formed out of an earlier work, more generally addressed to Christians and derived from TWT. This explains the tensions and contradictions, such as the implication that the reader might have children (whilst yet being a monk). Indeed, Battifol presents a largely convincing reconstruction of the underlying work which derives, he suggests, from the third century. Again, this is not inconceivable. Whether the extant *Syntagma* and the related *Fides patrum* are the result of the expansion of this original or the combination of this original with a monastic rule of distinct origin is a matter beyond this introduction.

Translations

The *Syntagma doctrinae*

1 ₁Such is the life of the sons of the catholic church and especially of those within her who are anchorites or monks. ₂We are being saved by grace, but grace desires that her own children should be sons of wisdom, self-selected and tested in every good deed, being

---

[7]Cf. Battifol, *Syntagma,* 158, who suggests that the direction on fasting on Wednesday and Friday and those regarding first-fruits are derived from *D*. However, if these are derived from *D* then these directions are taken out of sequence. It seems more probable that these regulations result not from a reading of *D* but from the widespread acceptance of fasting on Wednesday and Friday and the widespread reading of the laws regarding first-fruits as applying to Christians' charity.

zealous for the good and to act ₃so as to make themselves worthy of that correct faith, being careful, beloved, to guard these things. ₄They contend after loving the Lord your God with your whole heart and with your whole mind and your neighbour as yourself. ₅You shall not murder, you shall not commit adultery, you shall not fornicate, you shall not despoil a child, you shall not make potions, you shall not be troubled by mental division. ₆Abstain from anything strangled and from idolatry and from blood. ₇And those are the self-evident failings; the commandments which appear to be lesser, of which we shall give an account, are these. ₈To begin with those who are monks and celibates should keep apart from women and should neither approach them for conversation, nor hope, if possible, to see them lest they be penalized should the heart commit adultery through the vision of their eyes. ₉Be careful not to be double-worded or double-minded, not a liar, not talkative, not distracted, not shameless, not roaming, not unfeeling, not self-willed, not issuing a bad word from the lips, nor ever making an oath, but yes is yes and no is no. ₁₀If somewhere necessity comes about say, in conversation, "Know," or "I speak the truth" or "I do not lie." Do not take the venerable name upon an oath, nor anything else as an oath, as the Gospel said. ₁₁All those things are unfitting and improper to perform. But he expels from the church and condemns anyone who does not guard against them closely.

2   Do not make yourself naked in front of anyone, apart from the necessity of washing in sickness brought about through great weakness. ₂Do not call a brother "raka" or "fool". ₃Do not participate in the feasts of the nations. Do not keep sabbaths, ₄do not practise sorcery, do not make potions, nor do anything of this kind in disease or in the pain of suffering. ₅Do not depart in the direction of a spell, nor put a phylactery upon yourself, do not be a lustrator, neither doing such things yourself nor allowing another to do them to you. ₆Keep your body from any filth and licentiousness. ₇Do not have a woman living with you; just as some have accorded the names of beloved to themselves, yet rapidly have proved to be hateful. ₈Do not have coolness towards anyone, since the prayer of anyone who has coolness will not be acceptable to the Lord. ₉Do not pray with a heretic nor with gentiles. ₁₀Do not omit a fast, that is to say Wednesday and Friday, unless prevented by some illness, excepting only the Pentecost and the Epiphany. ₁₁And keep the forty days of the holy church and the week of the Holy Pascha carefully. ₁₂Relax the fast if a brother visits you, but not the mandated fast of the fourth (day), and Friday, and the forty days and the passion, but that of private election, on the second and third and fifth (days). ₁₃You should not fast on sabbath or Sunday, except for the great sabbath of the holy Pascha. ₁₄Fasting on the fourth (day) and the Friday is mandated until the ninth hour. ₁₅If you act additionally this is of your own choice; if you are able to do any supererogatory work you are practising asceticism nobly. ₁₆When you are fasting and conducting your life beware lest you be puffed-up, for puffing up is a snare of the devil, by which he fell from heaven, finally likewise he throws down humans thereby, as he entraps them. ₁₇Let nobody lead you astray into fasting on Sunday, not at all, nor to kneel at all, nor in the pentecost, for this is not an ordinance of the church. ₁₈And do not allow any Marcionites to lead you astray, or another heresy, into private fasting on the sabbath or on Sunday. ₁₉Do not neglect the meetings. ₂₀Prepare yourself thoroughly to be worthy of the mysteries, lest you assemble for judgement. ₂₁Do not neglect the washing of the feet of the brothers who come to you, for such a command shall be demanded of those who behave arrogantly towards it, even if they are bishops, for Our Lord himself first washed, commanding them to act thus.

3 Do not be money-loving, nor sordidly greedy, nor a lover of material goods, nor a lover of wealth. For they who are such cannot be pleasing to God. ₂Do not be engaged at all in business. ₃For there are many fields around unsown, and their inhabitants, not having a trade, are obliged to transact business; even if they are monastics they transact business, which is wrong except that necessity obliges.

₄Do not accept interest. ₅Do not buy up anything at lower than the accustomed price. ₆Love every person and make peace with all, even those with whom you do not pray, as much as you able, except on grounds of heresy. ₇Be one who will share with any who have not, and if you have not do not call in debts. ₈If anyone asks anything of you give it on loan and accept from him the capital, when he has it, without interest. ₉Do not deal treacherously before the Lord. ₁₀If you have possessions or money and anyone seeks to borrow from you, and if through not receiving interest you are obliged to sell things, it is more worthy should you trade at a fair price, that is cheaply, for God overpowers the wise in all their deeds. Look and observe that from one payment you may be receiving three or four times the return.

4   Be humble and peaceable, fearing always the sayings of the Lord. ₂Do not be antagonistic, do not strike anybody excepting only a child of yours, slightly, for the purpose of training, and then with moderation, being watchful lest somehow homicide come about through you, for many are the occasions of death. ₃Do not sneer at anyone at all. ₄Do not despise anyone on grounds of appearance. ₅Be moderate in clothing, not using soft clothes, not with your clothing appearing to be the dress of the righteous, that is not going about in rags. ₆If you are wearing sackcloth in sorrow for your sin see that your sackcloth is not apparent, but have it hidden within. ₇Neither should you wrap yourself in skins lest somehow you receive human glory. ₈Do not dress your hair at all, for the apostle forbids such an appearance, nor shave your beard, nor wear a tonsure when shaving.

5   If you are able to fast an entire week make no show of that to anyone. ₂Stay away from meat, not as though you dislike it, but withdrawing from food for the body, and considering yourself unworthy, and yearning for the heavenly, rather than the earthly. For anyone who is moderate in the enjoyment of food assists their own body towards continence. ₃Do not take wine at all, or simply taste (it) and bless the creator. If, like Timothy, you should be prone to illness through an extreme mode of life, use a little wine. For a little is a medicine for healing, whereas anyone who makes overmuch use is pushing himself into both weaknesses. So one cup, or two, but not more.

₄If you are able to go barefoot you will be regarded nobly. If you are obliged to shoe yourself at all your shoes should be simple, ₅and do not desire to be clad in decorated sandals of ponce-like form. ₆Be satisfied with what is at hand. And if you have a strict way of life with regard to meat and wine and depart abroad, do not desire to boast of yourself, but be the same as your brothers, inasmuch as you may make use of vegetables and soup. ₇If it is necessary to eat fish paste or to partake of fish, if you desire, do only this, and then take up your former asceticism. ₈If you are unwell, and eat an egg, it is no sin. ₉If you are weakened in an illness and should partake of poultry or meat, it is weakness for you, and is not reckoned a sin. Grieve because you have reduced your way of life and have slackened in your observance of the standard.

6   If in illness you are forced to, wash once or two times. If you are well you have no need of a bath. ₂You, who are a monastic and priest should take your rest on the ground if you are healthy. ₃Above all work at a trade. ₄Work in a field, so that you should not eat bread in idleness, ₅rather have possessions from your hands for the relief of brothers and strangers and if possible widows and orphans and the lowly. ₆And if you are living amongst people and have an inherited field or smallholding to work, there is no impropriety in gathering its fruits justly. First offer the first-fruits to the priests, then giving relief to widows and orphans and to others, from just labour, not from charging interest or from the affairs of greed or from extortion. ₇If you dwell at a cell do not be proud of the asceticism of the cell. ₈If you have gained your living from a smallholding and withdraw yourself to be an anchorite in a monastery you are not withdrawing but being foolish and are being deluded. ₉Do not desire to be idle living in a monastery, and be fed by others, but you should learn a trade or should labour, to obtain what you need. ₁₀If you have youngsters around you, principally be humble-minded and do not desire to be a teacher. ₁₁If you see souls being saved through your behaviour, being desirous of perfecting through doubling the five talents which you have accepted, care for the souls around you ₁₂and charge the youngsters each to seek solitude in conduct and behaviour, except at the table of the monastery and in the gathering and the psalmody. ₁₃In sleeping each should be wrapped on their own. And each should have their tunic or their sack so stowed that it may readily be found in the night. ₁₄Seek moderation in being wakeful for psalms and prayers, yet pray intensively during the days. ₁₅Do not draw out prayers and shout and babble, rather sing moderately so that the souls do not grow sick. ₁₆Be desirous that the children inclined to silence should advance. ₁₇You should not go into a tavern at all, but if necessity comes about when abroad and you have need of food or drink send to the market and eat it in the church and drink in the place set apart for this. ₁₈If there is no church in that place, nor a house of orthodox people, and there is necessity and you enter into a guesthouse, be sure to stay where there are no women or a bar, and that with regret.

7   Therefore, if you keep the commandments mentioned earlier and keep yourself from the errors mentioned earlier you will perfect your path in faith and in sanctity and in conduct, in accordance with what is said, shall obtain for yourself a great and good ascent. ₂These are the commandments and warnings of the faith mentioned earlier; if you perform them, and keep the faith, you shall be a disciple of Jesus Christ our Lord. ₃If anyone contradicts what is mentioned earlier he is contradicting God. He examines the divine Scriptures and understands the tradition of the church and he has understanding that the Lord gives commandment concerning all of these. ₄We, in order not to extend the discourse, shall not produce

testimonies. And these commandments are fitting for monastics and other Christians.

8 If any priest wishes to exercise the priesthood rigorously in accordance with the commandments mentioned earlier, he should be sober, serious, longsuffering, useful, a lover of orphans, a lover of the poor, a lover of strangers, a lover of good, peaceable, solid in faith and word and knowledge, keeping himself from women, not neglecting the flock, having no loathing of anyone, not respecting persons but reprimanding all. ₂Do not allow scabbed sheep in the flock but purify them through repentance and then herd them together in the pen. ₃It is necessary to know each as a pastor, what to announce to the widows, what to the monks, what to the laity, what to the catechumens those in chaste marriage, and this is not as though there were a different law, for there is one law for pastors. ₄Proclaim to women that they are not to speak in the church at all, but in all things to keep silence and to intercede, not to deck themselves in gold or raiment, not to show their face or kiss the hands of men. ₅Catechumens are to pray on their own, or outside the veil. ₆The whole people should hear the word of the Lord in fear and silence. ₇Not only should those who sin receive just punishment but those who rejoice in sin. ₈The priest should be vigilant concerning the sacrifices; for if he receives from a soldier who sheds blood, or a businessman, or one who swears oaths, or one who is wealthy through fraud, or one who exacts additional taxes, or a usurer, or one who raises prices on grain, or from any sinner, such a priest, if he receives from such, offers the blind and the lame to God from them. ₉It is not right that you, the laity, should judge the priest. Should you see him err, shun him. ₁₀If you keep these the priest shall obtain for himself a good ascent and great boldness in Christ Jesus our Lord, with whom to the Father together with the Holy Spirit be glory to the ages of the ages. Amen.

The *Fides patrum*

We believe in one God, the Father almighty, maker of all things visible and invisible, and in one Lord Jesus Christ the only begotten Son of God, begotten from the Father, that is from the being of the Father, God from God, light from light, true God from true God, begotten not made, one in being with the Father, through whom all things came about in the heavens and in the earth, who for us humans and for our salvation came down and was incarnate, suffering and rising on the third day, and ascending to the heavens, to come to judge the living and the dead. And in the Holy Spirit.

Those who say there was when he was not, and he was not before he was begotten, and that he came about from what was not or from any other substrate or being, saying that the Son of God is changeable or alterable, these the holy and catholic and apostolic church anathematizes from that holy faith which was set down in Nicaea by the holy fathers, for the illumination of the faithful and to make known the reason for each statement of those bishops, numbering 318, who agreed in it, moreover it being an ecumenical synod. So still following the faith set down we anathematize the faith of Sabellius which says that the Father and Son and the Holy Spirit are the same. For they are confused (saying) that the Father is as the Son, and that just as the Son is so is the Holy Spirit, such that they are a single person with three names. These are otherwise to the faith, for we know the Father to be the Father, the Son the Son and the Holy Spirit the Holy Spirit, one substance, one Kingdom. And we anathematize the faith of Photinus, which says that he is of Mary and is son in this way, and was not prior to this, but that it is apparently stated in the Scriptures that he is of Mary alone, even according to his divinity. These things we know to be otherwise to the faith, for the begotten Son was with the Father and in the Father, just as it is written. There was not a when when he was not the Son, but the Father always has a Son. For it is impossible for the Father to be without a Son so that he is subsequently called Father by advancement but he is always Father, always Son, as we said before, not as a twin brother, but he was begotten with the Father, as was written before. And as we believe of the Father and the Son, so we believe of the Holy Spirit, the divine Spirit, the Holy Spirit, the perfect Spirit, the Paraklete, uncreated, speaking in the law and prophets and apostles and descending onto the Jordan. Concerning the begetting of the Son we believe thus, that he took on perfect humanity from the virgin Mary, through the Holy Spirit, not from the seed of a man. Truly body and soul and not in appearance, for thus he wished perfectly to save humanity. And that he suffered, and that he was buried, and arose on the third day, and that he was taken up into the heavens and took his seat at the right hand of the Father, glorifying the humanity which he had taken, that he will come again to judge the living and the dead. If somehow the divine Scriptures apparently somehow speak of him as though of a creature, we accept that this was fulfilled according to the flesh. Still we anathematize those who do not confess the resurrection of the flesh, and all heresies opposed to that faith. Also the atheistic faith of the Arians has been anathematized in what has previously been written, namely that we believe that he was begotten and not made, for they say that the Son of God is a creation. For the completion of all the parts of the faith, we confess and say these things, that we believe in one baptism, in one church, in the resurrection of the flesh, in the Kingdom of the heavens, in everlasting judgment. We confess God as Father and Son and Holy Spirit, the Father incomprehensible, the Son incomprehensible, the Holy Spirit incomprehensible, for the Spirit is God, by his will and in truth and not in appearance appearing and speaking to the prophets and to the just, to Adam, to Noah, to Abraham, to Isaac, to Jacob, to Moses, to Joshua, to Samuel and to David, to Isaiah and to Elijah and to all the rest of the prophets, himself God of the old and the new. Insofar as Scripture speaks of the eye of the Lord, or the ears of the Lord, such things as Scripture says of God are true, as thus we believe incomprehensibly and inconceivably, and that humanity is entirely after the image of God.

1   The way of life of that catholic church, and especially of bishops and clerks and monastics and other Christians and of all their sons. They should command firstly in this way, directing and stating thus: that we are saved by grace, but grace desires that her own children should be self-selected and sons of wisdom, and tested in every good deed, to be zealous for the good and so to act, manifestly to make themselves worthy of that correct faith, and to guard these, after that they should love the Lord God from all the heart and soul, and the neighbour as themselves, that we should not murder, that we should not commit adultery, that we should not fornicate, that we should not make potions, that we should not despoil a child, that we should not steal, that we should not bear false witness, that we should not be troubled by mental division. That we should abstain from anything strangled and from blood. Beware, man, lest anyone deceive you away from this faith, since they are instructing you apart from God. And those are the evident failings; those commandments which appear to be slightest, of which we shall give an account, are those. To begin with those who are monks and celibates keep apart from women, and should neither approach them for conversation, nor hope, if possible, to see them lest they be penalized as the heart commits adultery. They should take care not to be double-tongued or double-minded, not a liar, not talkative, not improperly acting, not roaming, not shameless, not unfeeling, not self-willed nor issuing a bad word, nor ever making an oath, but yes is yes and no is no. And if, somewhere, you should be engaged in conversation, know that you should say "I speak the truth and do not lie." Do not take the venerable name upon an oath, nor anything else as an oath, as the Gospel said. Such errors are unsuitable and unfitting, but expel from the church anyone who does not guard against them closely and condemn them.

2   Do not make yourself naked in front of anyone, except in necessity, in washing or in sickness, or when in need of the waters. Do not call any brother a raka, or a fool. Do not participate in the feasts of the gentiles. Do not observe sabbaths as do the Jews, do not practise sorcery, do not make potions, nor do anything else in disease or suffering or pain or hurt. Do not depart in the direction of a spell, nor put phylacteries upon yourself, do not be a lustrator, neither doing such things yourself nor allowing others to do them to you. Keep your body from any filth and licentiousness. Do not have a woman living with you; just as some have accorded the names of beloved to themselves, yet rapidly have proved to be hateful. Do not have coolness towards anyone, since your prayer will not be acceptable to the Lord. Do not gather with heretics or with gentiles. Do not omit the fast of the Lord, that is to say Wednesday and Friday, unless prevented by some illness, excepting only the Pentecost and the holy Epiphany. And keep the week of the Holy Pascha, being very careful not to slacken the fast; if a brother visits you, share an agape with him; the fast of which I speak is not that mandated for the fourth (day), and Friday, and the forty days, but that of private election, on the second and third and fifth (days). Do not fast on the sabbath for the whole day, for it is improper that you should fast the whole day on the sabbath until the setting of the sun, that is until the sixth or the seventh hour. The sun should not set upon you while you fast, as Sunday is coming on. It is mandated that the fast of the fourth (day) and the Friday is until the ninth hour. If you do anything additional you are performing this of your own choice; if you are able to do any supererogatory work you shall have a greater reward. When you are fasting thus, and striving, be careful not to become puffed-up, for puffing up is a snare of the devil, by which he fell from heaven, and likewise he throws down humans thereby, as he entraps them. Let nobody at all ever lead you astray into fasting on Sunday, nor to kneel on Sunday, nor in the pentecost, for this is not an ordinance of the church. And lest any Marcionites lead you astray, or another heresy, into fasting on the sabbath, do not neglect the meetings. Prepare yourself thoroughly to be worthy of the undefiled mysteries, lest you should bring judgement on yourself. Do not neglect the washing of the feet of the brothers who come to you, for such a command shall be demanded of those who behave arrogantly towards it, even if they are bishops, for the Lord of these first bathed the feet of the disciples, commanding them to act thus.

3   Do not be money-loving, nor sordidly greedy, nor super-wealthy, Do not desire to gain silver or gold, except only as a means of obtaining food and clothing. For the friends of mammon cannot also be pleasing as servants to God. Do not be engaged at all in business. For there are many fields around unsown, and their inhabitants, not having a trade, are obliged to transact business; even if they are monastics they transact business, which is wrong except out of necessity. Do not accept interest. Do not purchase at less than the accustomed price. Love every person and make peace with all except heretics. Be one who shares with any who have not, and if you have not do not call in debts. If anyone asks a loan of you give it and accept from him the capital, and only when he has it. Do not deal treacherously before the Lord. If you have possessions or money and anyone seeks to borrow from you, and if through not receiving interest you are obliged to sell things, it is more worthy should you trade at a fair price, that is cheaply, for God grabs the wise in all their operation. Look and observe that from one payment you may be receiving three or four times the return.

4   Be humble and peaceable, fearing always the sayings of the Lord. Do not be antagonistic, do not strike anybody excepting only a child of yours, slightly, for the purpose of training, and then with moderation. Be watchful lest somehow homicide come about through you, for the occasions of death are many. Do not sneer at anyone, nor despise anyone on grounds of appearance. Be moderate in clothing, not using soft clothes, not appearing to be righteous in your clothing, that is not going about in rags. If you are wearing sackcloth in sorrow for your sin see that your sackcloth is not apparent, but have it hidden within, lest you receive human glory. Do not dress your hair at all, for the apostle forbids such an appearance, nor shave your beard, nor wear a tonsure.

5 If you are able to pass an entire week in fasting make no show of that to anyone. Stay away from meat, not as though you dislike it, but withdrawing from food for the body, and obliged to consider yourself unworthy, and yearning for the heavenly, rather than the earthly. For anyone who is moderate in the enjoyment of food assists their own body towards continence. Above all do not take wine, except to taste and to bless the creator. If, like the honourable Timothy, you should be prone to illness through overmuch continence, use a little wine. For a little is a medicine for healing, whereas anyone who makes overmuch use is pushing himself into both weaknesses. So one cup, or two, but not more. If you are able to go barefoot you will be acting nobly. If you are obliged to be shod at all your shoes should be simple, and do not desire to be shod in decorated sandals of ponce-like form. And if you have a way of life excluding meat and wine and depart abroad, do not desire to boast of yourself, but be the same as your brothers, in using vegetables and soup. If it is necessary to eat fish paste or to partake of fish, if you desire, do only this. If you are unwell, and eat an egg, it is no sin. If you are weakened in an illness and should eat of poultry or meat, it is weakness for you, do not reckon it a sin. Be grieved because you have reduced your way of life and have slackened in your observance of the standard.

6 If in illness you are forced to wash, [do so] once or twice. If you are well you have no need. You, who are a monastic and priest should take your rest on the ground if you are healthy. Above all know a trade, or work in a field, so that you should not eat bread in idleness, bur rather should have possessions from your hands to share with brothers and strangers and widows and orphans. And if you are living amongst people[8] and have an inherited field or smallholding, there is no impropriety in gathering its fruits justly. First offer the

---

[8]Batiffol reads "Among strangers."

first-fruits to the priests, then give relief to widows and orphans and to brothers besides, from just labour, not from charging interest or from the affairs of greed. If you dwell in a cell do not be proud of the asceticism of the cell. If you get your living from a smallholding and withdraw to be an anchorite in a monastery you are not withdrawing but being foolish and are being deluded. Do not desire to be idle living in a monastery, and be fed by others, but you should have a trade or should labour, to gain what you need. If you have youngsters around you above all be humble-minded and do not desire to be a teacher. If you see souls being saved through you, being desirous of perfecting through doubling the five talents which you have accepted, care for the souls around you and charge the youngsters each to seek solitude in your conduct and your life together, except at the table of the monastery and in the gathering for psalmody. In sleeping each should be wrapped on their own. And each should have their own tunic or their sack stowed so that it may readily be found in the night. Observe wakefulness in psalms and prayers and hymns in moderation. Do not draw out prayers and babble, rather sing moderately so that the souls do not grow sick. Be desirous that the children should progress silently. Avoid taverns absolutely, but if necessity comes about when you are abroad and you have need of food or drink send to the market and eat it in the church and drink in the place set apart for this. If there is no church in that place, or a house of orthodox people, and there is necessity and you enter a guesthouse, be sure to stay where there are no women or a bar, and that with regret. As far as is in your power do not pray alongside those who are found in the theatre or the racetrack or the hunt. If there is some necessity and you are gathered with the mighty, those who are consorting with them shall be seen, so you should be on your guard against them.

7   And these commandments are suitable for monks, and ascetics, and for widows, and for Christian people who are living in a chaste marriage.

8   If any priest or any other of the clerics should wish to guard the priesthood rigorously, to be sober, serious, longsuffering, valuable, a lover of orphans, a lover of the poor, a lover of good, conciliatory, solid in faith and word and knowledge, keeping himself from women, principally he should be eager for the church, and in not neglecting the flock, having no loathing of anyone, not fastidious, not greedy. In accordance with the dictum of the apostle, not respecting persons in upbraiding the small and the great for any fault, friend and stranger alike. Do not allow scabby sheep in the flock but purify them from sins through repentance and afterwards herd them together in the pen, that is in the church. For pastoring it is necessary to know each, what to announce to the widows, what to the laity, what to the catechumens, what to the monastics, what to those in chaste marriage, and this is not as though there were a different law, for there is one law for pastors. Proclaim to women that they are not to speak in the church, not even in a whisper, nor to sing along, but solely to keep silence and to beseech God through intercession and a chaste way of life. Not to have from themselves bright raiment, nor gold dresses or jewellery, not to show their faces, neither in the marketplace nor in the church. Not to kiss the hands of men, unless they are elderly or aging or elders and very faithful.

And these are the saving instructions of the holy 318 fathers, which lead the way to the eternal life of God, to whom be the glory and the power to the ages of ages. Amen.[9]

The Coptic conclusion:

Catechumens are to pray on their own, or outside the veil. The whole people should pray in fear and trembling, hearing the word of the Lord in silence.

[9]This is the conclusion of the Greek text. The Coptic text continues. Given that it reflects the text of the *Syntagma* it may provide a guide to the missing contents, though the conclusion of this version is itself uncertain as the MS is lacunose.

If anyone speaks during a reading, he is showing contempt for the word of the Lord and will not give a good account of himself. Moreover this blame will affect the leaders. For those who sin do not render an account solely to the Lord, but all those who are in agreement with them, even if they have not sinned themselves but rejoiced in others who sin. That is why the same sentence of condemnation is theirs.

Regarding those who touch the offerings, it is proper for the priest of God to be prudent and moderate, not to show contempt for his rights to the first-fruits of foodstuffs. For if he receives from a soldier who sheds blood, from one who causes loss to another, or from a prefect, or from a businessman who swears oaths for shameful gain, or from a general, accursed by those he has violated, or from a violent rich person who is violent to his servants and does not feed them, or clothe them, or from a murderer of from a thief, especially if they are unrepentant, or from somebody who practises usury with regard to his debtors, or idolaters, or magicians, or incanters, or those who go to pagan gatherings, or are effeminate, or artists who sculpt or paint the images of idols, or tricksters and forgers who use fake weights, or money changers, or drunkards or tavern keepers, or from false priests. If the priest of God receives offerings from any of them, or allows any group of sinners into the temple, he is not in conformity with those things which we have said, and if he does not avoid those things which we have proscribed, anything he offers at the altar of the Lord is lame and blind. He is taking the fault upon himself, and he is polluting the house of the Lord, because he has not preferred to the Lord and his temple to his own wellbeing.

But whoever believes shall be faithful to the Lord and to his Christ. Glory to the Father and the Son and the Holy Spirit, in all the ages of the ages. Amen.

Part three: The rule of St Benedict

Introduction

The *Rule of St Benedict* was a rule for monks within the western church, written by Benedict in the sixth century, though certainly based in part on earlier sources, in particular an anonymous monastic rule known as the *Rule of the Master*. In the fourth chapter, that translated here, we find a set of precepts which are not specifically monastic but seem to be addressed, rather as the material underlying the pseudo-Athanasian documents, to Christians more generally. There is an extensive discussion of this material in van de Sandt and Flusser's book on **D**, and it is sufficient here to repeat their conclusion that this material had found its way into monastic rules in the west, much as it did in the east, as a result of the employment of two-ways material in baptismal catechesis.[10] It is likewise clear that this is not a direct rendition of any particular extant version of the tradition, but the weight of the parallels indicates that this is not simply an independent version of the material derived directly from Scripture.

Translation

What are the instruments of good works?

First of all to love the Lord God with the whole heart, the whole soul, the whole strength, then one's neighbour as oneself. Then, not to kill, not to commit adultery, not to steal, not to covet, not to bear false witness, to honour all people, and that one should not do to another what one would not have done to oneself. To deny one's self in order to follow Christ. To discipline the body, not to seek pleasure, to love fasting, to relieve the poor, to clothe the naked, to visit the

[10]H. van de Sandt and D. Flusser, *The Didache*, 90–95.

sick, to bury the dead, to support those in trouble, to console the grieving, to distance oneself from the activities of the world, to prefer nothing to the love of Christ. Not to give way to anger, not to foster a desire for revenge, not to entertain deceit in the heart, not to make a false peace, not to forsake charity, not to swear an oath, lest by chance one swear falsely, to speak the truth with heart and tongue, not to return evil for evil, not to inflict any injury, but patiently to suffer any inflicted on oneself, to love one's enemies, not to return a curse for a curse, but rather to bless, to bear persecution for the sake of justice. Not to be proud, not to be given to wine, not to be greedy, not to be drowsy, not to be lazy, not to be a grumbler, not to be a complainer, to put one's trust in God, to attribute to God any good one sees in oneself, and not to oneself, but to know that any evil is one's own, and to blame oneself for it. To fear the day of judgement, to dread hell, to desire eternal life with all spiritual longing, daily to keep death before one's eyes, to keep constant watch over our lives' activities, to know with certainty that God looks upon us in every place, to dash at once against Christ any wicked thoughts that come into one's heart and to disclose them to our spiritual father, and to guard one's mouth against any wicked and profane speech. Not to love garrulity, not to speak pointless words nor such as to provoke laughter, not to love much or boisterous laughter, gladly to hear sacred readings, to apply oneself to prayer frequently, daily to confess to God one's former offences with sighs and tears, and to amend our lives from such evils. Not to put into effect the desires of the flesh, to despise one's own will, in all things to obey the demands of the abbot, even should he, which should not happen, act otherwise, mindful of that statement of the Lord "Do what they say, do not do what they do." (Mt 23.3). Not to desire to be called holy before one actually is, but firstly to be holy so that one may rightly be so called, daily to fulfill the demands of the Lord in what one does, to love chastity, to hate nobody, not to be jealous, not to entertain envy, not to love quarrels, to flee from pride, to honour the aged, to love the young, to pray for one's enemies in the love of Christ, to make peace with those with whom one has disagreed before the sun sets, and never to despair of the mercy of God.

These are the instruments of the spiritual art. If they have been fulfilled unceasingly by us, night and day, and on the day of judgement are approved, they will obtain for us the reward from God which he himself promised, which eye has not seen, nor ear heard, which God has prepared for those who love him (1 Cor 2.9). But the workshop in which we perform all this diligently is the enclosure of the monastery, and stability in the community.

CHAPTER FIVE

TWT in the later western tradition

With the monastic adaptations of TWT the literary history of the tradition in the east comes to its conclusion. *D* was adapted to become part of the *Apostolic Constitutions*, but this does not constitute a chapter in the history of TWT as the presence of the material there is the result of this literary collection, which effectively marks the conclusion of the living use of the tradition. The same may be said of the brief citations of TWT in the *Sentences* of Isaac the Syrian and in the *Fragmenta Anastasiana* which make allusions to TWT but are in any event ultimately dependent on *Apostolic Constitutions*.[1] It is perhaps through the dominating influence of the *Apostolic Constitutions* that the tradition ceases to live.

In the west, however, as not only the work of Lactantius observed at the beginning of chapter four above but also the continued circulation of *L*, the tradition lived on. Thus we leave the trail with two further adaptations of TWT in the western tradition; in which the catechetical roots of the tradition are still manifest.

---

[1]The *Fragmenta Anastasiana* may be found in F.X. Funk, *Didascalia et constitutiones apostolorum* II (Paderborn: Schoeningh, 1905), 50–71, the *Sentences* of Isaac in Marius Besson, "Un recueil de sentences attribué à Isaac le Syrien," *Oriens Christianus* 1 (1901), 46–60, 288–298.

Part one: ps-Boniface, fifteenth homily

Introduction

This sermon is preserved in the two Latin manuscripts in which *L* has been transmitted, indicating that the scribes observed the relationship between the documents. These manuscripts are collections of homilies, and the sermon here is appended to the collection, not being set for a particular day in the liturgical year, but clearly intended as a homily on the renunciation at baptism. It is also found independently in a Vatican manuscript, *Pal. Lat.* 485, from which the following version is translated.

Echoes of the TWT occur throughout, though it would be an error to suggest that it is directly based on any other model, but is rather the fruit of a living tradition. The manuscript was written before 875, which provides the latest possible date for the sermon itself, and although addressed to those who have already been baptized its simple teaching implies that it has been preached in a context in which paganism is still alive and in which evangelization is a relatively recent event.[2]

Translation

Listen, brothers, and give careful thought to what you renounced at baptism. For you renounced the devil and all his works. These are works of his which you renounced: pride, envy, malice, slander, lying, perjury, fornication, adultery, murder, theft, false witness, robbery, avarice, greed, drunkenness, obscene speech, quarrels, rage, poisonings, sorceries, consultation of fortune-tellers; belief in witches and werewolves, disobedience to your masters, the wearing of amulets. These and wicked deeds like to them belong to the devil.

[2]Much more extensive discussion may be found at Van de Sandt and Flusser, *Didache*, 95–107.

All these you renounced at baptism. As the Apostle says: "those who do such things" deserve death and "shall not inherit the kingdom of God." (Gal 5.21) But we believe that through the mercy of God you have renounced all these wicked acts, listed above, with your heart and deed and that you have changed through confession and fitting penitence so that you might deserve to acquire the reward. So you promised at baptism and so you should keep these promises. First of all, you promised to believe in God the almighty Father and in Jesus Christ his Son and in the Holy Spirit, who is one almighty God in perfect Trinity.

Thus these are the commandments of God which you should perform and keep: that you should love the same God whom you have confessed with all your heart, with all your soul, with all your strength and with all your mind. Then your neighbours as your-selves, because the whole law, and the prophets, hangs on these two commandments. Be patient, be merciful, kind, chaste, undefiled. Teach your sons and daughters that they should fear God. Likewise your slaves.[3] Reconcile those who are in disagreement. Judge justly. Do not accept unjust gifts because gifts blind even the wise. Keep the Lord's day. Gather at the church to pray there, and not to chatter. Give alms according to your ability. Be hospitable to one another, receive strangers, visit the sick, support widows and orphans. Give tithes to the churches, and do not do to another what you would not want done to you. Fear God alone, everywhere. Servants, be subject to your masters.

Hold fast to the Lord's Prayer and the creed which is "I believe in God". And pass it on to your children and your little ones whose sponsors you become in baptism. Rejoice in fasting, love righteous-ness, resist the devil always, receive the eucharist at the right times. These are the works which God commands you to perform and observe, with those like them. Believe that Christ will come, and in the resurrection of the flesh and in the judgement of all, when the

---

[3] The manuscript reads "daughter." The translation suggests an emendation from *filiam* to *familiam*.

evil will be separated from the just and sent into everlasting fire, and the just into everlasting life. There is life with God, without death, there is everlasting glory without end. There the just shall shine forth like the sun, there are all the good things which the eye has not seen, nor the ears heard, which have arisen in a human heart, which God has prepared for those who love him, (1 Cor 2.9) and which he deigns to provide, he who lives and reigns in a perfect Trinity, God for ever and ever. Amen.

PART TWO: THE SECOND CATECHESIS OF THE MANNER OF CATECHIZING CONVERTS

Introduction

In the eighth century missions from England to the Franks sought conversion to Christianity. Since this policy was supported by the emerging Holy Roman Empire it seems that converts were being made at a great rate, but that the missionaries were poorly equipped to bring about conversion of the heart. This homily is one of six, on different topics, intended for the instruction of converts, and guidance for their instructors. Whereas this catechesis concentrates on the commandments there are echoes of the tradition in the expression of the commandments and in the manner in which the commandments are linked to the golden rule and to an eschatological promise. We may surmise that the anonymous author had drawn upon the tradition in producing this homily.

We so leave the tradition on the fringes of the Christian world, in a world utterly altered from that in which the tradition had been formed, but in which neither the desire to make disciples for the triumphant Lord of Israel nor the need to equip these disciples to keep their baptismal covenant in a hostile world was in any way diminished.

Translation

Concerning the ten commandments of the law

If you totally desire to be a Christian, you can escape the great darknesses of ignorance and faithlessness. For if you can keep the directions of the divine law you shall really be a Christian. If anyone replies that he is able to keep them you will say to him: "It is good indeed to promise, but your task is to keep your promise which God, who is present everywhere, hears. See, then, that you hold to what you are going to hear. The almighty God who made us 'in his image and after his likeness' (Gen 1.26), himself gave us the law so that we might know in what way we should live and worship God.

Thus he spoke by means of his holy servant Moses: 'You shall not worship idols, you shall not murder, you shall not commit adultery, you shall not bear false witness, you shall not steal, you shall not work magic, you shall not foretell events neither from mountains, nor from trees, nor from fountains, nor from rivers. You will not make sacrifices in remote places, nor in any other place, rather carry your sacrifice to the holy church, and there the servants of God may offer for you a sacrifice to God alone as for those of yours who wish to become Christians, and you may beseech the mercy of God for your present welfare and eternal salvation. Honour your father, and your mother. You shall love the Lord your God with all your heart and with all your recollection and with all your mind, more than yourself. Because if you love God from the depths of your heart then you will indeed be loving yourself because this (life) is passing. But because of eternal life and your salvation you should love both God and yourself. Next you shall love your neighbour as yourself. And whatever you would not want done to you, do not do to any other. And do not begrudge anyone whatever good you would want done to yourself.'

These are the ten commands of the law of God, which lead all people who observe them to such glory and to such blessedness and to such blessedness which nobody can see with eyes of flesh, nor hear with ears of flesh, nor can any tongue express, which are so great and so many, which God has prepared for those who love him. (1 Cor 2.9) Hence you should labour with care and with great perseverance at keeping these commands, and at deserving such good things by pleasing God. For he is ready to give them not only to you but to all who truly worship him and truly believe in him. Almighty God, who lives and reigns for ever."

Bibliography

Aldridge, R.E., "The Lost Ending of the Didache", *Vigiliae Christianae* 53 (1999), 1–15.

Altaner, Berthold, "Zum Problem der lateinischen Doctrina Apostolorum" *Vigiliae Christianae*, 6 (1952), 160–167.

Amélineau, E., *Monuments pour servir à l'histoire de l'Égypte chrétienne aux IVᵉ et Vᵉ siècles* (Paris: Ernest Leroux, 1888).

Audet, J-P, "Affinités littéraires et doctrinales du 'Manuel de discipline'" *Revue Biblique* 59 (1952), 219–238.

Balzer, Klaus, *The Covenant Formulary in Old Testament, Jewish and Early Christian Writings* (Oxford: Basil Blackwell, 1971).

Battifol, P., *Didascalia CCCXVIII patrum* (Paris: Ernest Leroux, 1887).

———, *Syntagma doctrinae* (Studia patristica 2; Paris: Ernest Leroux, 1890).

Besson, Marius, "Un recueil de sentences attribué à Isaac le Syrien" *Oriens Christianus* 1 (1901), 46–60, 288–298.

Carleton Paget, James, *The Epistle of Barnabas: Outlook and Background* (WUNT 2.64; Tübingen: Mohr-Siebeck, 1994).

Draper, Jonathan A., "A continuing enigma: The 'yoke of the Lord' in Didache 6:2–3 and Early Jewish-Christian Relations". In P. J. Tomson and D. Lambers-Petry (eds), *The Image of Judaeo-Christians in Ancient Jewish and Christian Literature* (Tübingen: Mohr Siebeck, 2003), 106–123.

———, "Barnabas and the riddle of the Didache revisited" *JSNT* 58 (1995), 89–113.

———, "Torah and Troublesome Apostles in the Didache Community," *Novum Testamentum* 33 (1991), 347–372.

Faivre, A., "La documentation canonico-liturgique de l'église ancienne" *RevSR* 54 (1980), 204–219, 273–297.

Funk, F.X., *Didascalia et constitutiones apostolorum* II (Paderborn: Schoeningh, 1905).

Garrow, Alan, *The Gospel of Matthew's Dependence on the* Didache (London: T&T Clark, 2004).

Gebhardt, O. et al. (edd.), *Patrum apostolicorum opera* 1.2 (Leipzig: Hinrichs, 1878).

Goodspeed, E.J., "The Didache, Barnabas and the Doctrina" *Anglican Theological Review* 27 (1945), 228–247.

Harnack, Adolf von, *Die Apostellehre und die jüdischen beiden Wege* (Lepizig: Hinrichs, 1886).

Hennecke, E., "Die Grundschrift der Didache und ihre Recensionen", *ZNW* 2 (1901), 58–72.

Kloppenborg, John S., "Poverty and Piety in Matthew, James and the Didache" in Huub van de Sandt and Jürgen K. Zangenberg (edd.) *Matthew, James and the Didache: Three Related Documents in their Jewish and Christian Settings* (Atlanta: SBL, 2008), 201–232.

Kraft, R.A., *The Apostolic Fathers 3: Barnabas and the Didache* (New York: Nelson, 1965).

Krawutzcky, A., "Über das altkirchliche Unterrichtsbuch 'Die zwei Wege oder die Entscheidung des Petrus'" *ThQ* 64 (1882), 359–445.

Lockett, D.R., "Structure or Communicative Strategy? The 'Two Ways' motif in James' theological instruction" *Neotestamentica* 42 (2008) 269–287.

Loman, J., "The Letter of Barnabas in early second-century Egypt" in A. Hilhorst and G.H. van Kooten (edd.) *The Wisdom of Egypt: Jewish, Early Christian and Gnostic Essays in Honour of Gerard P. Luttikhuizen* (Leiden: Brill, 2005), 247–265.

Martínez, Florentino García and Eibert J.C. Tigchelaar, *The Dead Sea Scrolls: Study Edition* I (Leiden: Brill, 1997).

Milavec, A., *The Didache: Faith, Hope, & Life of the Earliest Christian Communities, 50–70 C.E.*, (New York: Paulist, 2003).

Niederwimmer, K., *The Didache* (Minneapolis: Fortress, 1998).

Peterson, E., "Über einige Probleme der Didache-Überlieferung" in *Frühkirche, Judentum und Gnosis* (Rome: Herder, 1959), 146–182.

Prigent, Pierre, R.A. Kraft, *Épître de Barnabé* (Paris: Cerf, 1971).

Robinson, J.A., *Barnabas, Hermas and the Didache* (London: SPCK, 1920).

Rordorf, Willy, "An Aspect of the Judeo-Christian Ethic: The Two Ways" in J.A. Draper (ed.) *The* Didache *in Modern Research* (Leiden: Brill, 1996), 148–164.

_____, A. Tuilier, *La doctrine des douze apôtres* (2nd ed.; Paris: Cerf, 1998).

Sanders, E.P., "Jewish Associations with Gentiles and Galatians 2.11–14" in R.T. Fortna and B.R. Gaventa (edd.) *The Conversation Continues* (Nashville: Abingdon, 1990), 170–88.

Schermann, Theodor, *Eine Elfapostelmoral oder die X-Rezension der "beiden Wege"* (Munich: Lentner, 1903).

Slee, Michelle, *The Church in Antioch in the First Century CE* (London: T&T Clark, 2003.

Stewart-Sykes, Alistair, *The Apostolic Church Order* (Sydney: St Paul's, 2006).

_____, "The Word and the Sweet Scent: A Rereading of the *stinoufi* Prayer of the Coptic Didache" *Anaphora* 1 (2007), 53–64.

van de Sandt, Huub, "Didache 3,1–6: A Transformation of an Existing Jewish Hortatory Pattern", *Journal for the Study of Judaism* 23 (1992) 21–41.

_____, "James 4,1–4 in the Light of the Jewish Two Ways Tradition 3,1–6." *Bib* 88 (2007) 38–63.

_____, "Law and Ethics in Matthew's Antitheses and James's Letter: A Reorientation of Halakah in Line with the Jewish Two Ways 3:1–6," in H. van de Sandt and J. Zangenberg (eds.), *Matthew, James and Didache: Three Related Documents in their Jewish and Christian Settings* (Atlanta: SBL, 2008), 315–338.

_____, and D. Flusser, *The Didache: Its Jewish Sources and its Place in Early Judaism and Christianity* (Assen: Van Gorcum, 2002)

Zetterholm, Magnus, *The Formation of Christianity at Antioch* (London: Routledge, 2003).

POPULAR PATRISTICS SERIES

ST VLADIMIR'S SEMINARY PRESS
1-800-204-2665 • www.svspress.com